POETRY BY BARBARA HOWES

The Blue Garden, Wesleyan University Press, 1972
Looking Up At Leaves, Alfred A. Knopf, 1966
Light And Dark, Wesleyan University Press, 1959
In The Cold Country, Bonacio and Saul, with Grove Press, 1954
The Undersea Farmer, Banyan Press, 1948

EDITED BY BARBARA HOWES

The Eye Of The Heart: Short Stories From Latin America,
Bobbs-Merrill, 1973

The Sea-Green Horse: Short Stories For Young People,
(with Gregory Jay Smith), Macmillan, 1966

From The Green Antilles: Writings Of The Caribbean,
Macmillan, 1966

23 Modern Stories, Vintage Books, 1963

A Private Signal

*Poems
New and Selected*

A PRIVATE SIGNAL

Poems New & Selected

by

Barbara Howes

Wesleyan University Press
Middletown, Connecticut

Acknowledgment is gratefully made to the following, in the pages of
which most of the new poems in this book were first published: *Choomia,
Poems From France, Poems From Italy, The Southern Review, Virginia Quarterly Review,* and *Weid.* "Equestrian Statue" is from *Cántico:
A Selection* by Jorge Guillén. Edited by Norman Thomas di Giovanni.
Copyright © 1965 by Jorge Guillén and Norman Thomas di Giovanni.
Reprinted by permission of Little, Brown and Company in association
with The Atlantic Monthly Press. Acknowledgment is also made to
the publishers of the books from which these poems were selected, and to
the editors of the periodicals in which the poems were first published.

Library of Congress Cataloging in Publication Data
Howes, Barbara.
  A private signal.
  I. Title.
PS3515.0924P7   811'.5'4   77-74559
ISBN 0-8195-5013-2
ISBN 0-8195-6051-0 pbk.

Manufactured in the United States of America
First edition

for Eleanor
and for Red Warren

CONTENTS

In the Cold Country

from The Blue Garden

Away

Eight Translations

New Poems

from
Light and Dark

Light and Dark

for
Harriott Allen

Chimera

After a fearful maze where doubt
Crept at my side down the terrible lightless channel,
I came in my dream to a sandspit parting
Wind-tossed fields of ocean. There,
Lightstepping, appeared
A trio of moose or mules
Ugly as peat,
Their trotters slim as a queen's.
"Hippocampi!" cried a voice as they sped
Over black water, their salty course,
And away. From the heaving sea
Then sprang a fabulous beast
For its evening gallop.
Head of a lion, goat's head rearing
Back, derisive, wild — the dragon
Body scaling in the waves; each reckless
Nature in balance, flying apart
In one. How it sported
Across the water, how it ramped and ran!
My heart took heart. Awaking, I thought:
What was disclosed in this vision
Was good; phantom or real,
I have looked on a noble animal.

Early Supper

Laughter of children brings
    The kitchen down with laughter.
While the old kettle sings
Laughter of children brings
To a boil all savory things.
    Higher than beam or rafter,
Laughter of children brings
    The kitchen down with laughter.

So ends an autumn day,
    Light ripples on the ceiling,
Dishes are stacked away;
So ends an autumn day,
The children jog and sway
    In comic dances wheeling.
So ends an autumn day,
    Light ripples on the ceiling.

They trail upstairs to bed,
    And night is a dark tower.
The kettle calls: instead
They trail upstairs to bed,
Leaving warmth, the coppery-red
    Mood of their carnival hour.
They trail upstairs to bed,
    And night is a dark tower.

To W. H. Auden
on his Fiftieth Birthday

Books collide—
Or books in a library do:
Marlowe by Charlotte Mew,
Sir Horace Walpole by Hugh;
The most unlikely writers stand shoulder to shoulder;
One studies incongruity as one grows older.

Symbols collide—
Signs of the zodiac
Range the celestial track,
Pisces has now swung back
Into the lead: we learn to recognize
Each fleck for what it is in our mackerel skies.

Ideas collide—
As words in a poem can.
The poet, Promethean,
Strikes fire in a single line,
Form glows in the far reaches of his brain;
Poets who travel will come home again.

Feeling collides—
Lying for years in wait,
May grope or hesitate.
Now let us celebrate
Feeling, ideas, symbols, books which can
Meet with greatness here within one man.

Danaë

Golden, within this golden hive
Wild bees drone,
As if at any moment they may
Swarm and be gone
From the arched fibres of their cage,
Lithe as whalebone.

Over a pasture, once, I saw
A flock of small
Martins flying in concert, high
Then wheeling, fall;
Like buckshot pent in a string bag
They dotted all

That sky-patch, holding form in their flight,
A vase poured,
Their breathing shape hung in the air—
Below, the road
Fled secretly as quicksilver:
My eyes blurred.

All things come to their pinnacle
Though landscapes shift,
Women sit in the balance, as
Upon a knife;
Irony cuts to the quick—is this
Life or new life?

They sit their years out on a scale,
The heavy yoke
Of their heavy stomachs grounding them —
Or else come back
To barrenness with each full moon;
Minds go slack

Longing, or dreading, that a new
Form will take shape.
(The martins' swarming is a brush-stroke
On the landscape,
Within their white-gold, fleshly hall
The wild bees wake.)

Homing at close of day, they meet
This moment: now:
Love calls from its subterranean passage,
The bed they know
May support agony or joy —
To bed they go.

Midwinter Flight

Enclosed within its journey, the plane
Lies like the hull of a ship balanced
On ways of air, a war canoe
Jutting into the dark,
A radiant toy
Loosed upon space.
     Here in this great cocoon
We passengers are pharaohs walled up
With honey, ambergris, grain and silver
To solace our hibernation.
Or we may be
Glazed ceramic fruit, a still-life
Kept for some later century
Under glass.
     Now while the plane
Tunnels the black massif, we think of other
Things: a circular stair,
Drums, a crimson maple, rainfall, hills,
And checkered moths
Trembling on a lighted pane.

Cat on Couch

My cat, washing her tail's tip, is a whorl
Of white shell,
As perfect as a fan
In full half-moon . . . Next moment she's a hare:
The muzzle twitches, blurs, goes dumb, and one
Tall ear dips, falters forward . . . Then,
Cross as switches, she's a great horned owl;
Two leafy tricorned ears reverse, a frown
Darkens her chalky visage, big eyes round
And round and stare down midnight.
There sits my cat

Mysterious as gauze, — now somnolent,
Now jocose, quicksilver from a dropped
Thermometer. When poised
Below the sketched ballet-
Dancers who pirouette upon the wall,
Calmly she lifts the slim
Boom of her leg, what will
The prima ballerina next
Perform? — Grace held in readiness,
She meditates, a vision of repose.

Lignum Vitæ

There in Bologna eighty saints are lodged
On pedestals, in rows up
The vaulted ceiling, till
Heads meet at the top
Of the hall.

Statues can wither like a blighted tree,
The hand holding the pen suffers
Dry rot, and a mantle embroidered
So skillfully
On oak

Disappears. Indeed, it is our loss
Not to have lived five hundred years
Ago, when in their vigor
These figures were all
One color.

A controversy now in black and white,
The restored saints look down: one's right
Hand is clean new pine,
Another's torso
Speckled

As a mosaic. Near the end is an old man
Reading a new book; his robe
Flows yet from broad shoulders
Without break
Or stain.

For a Florentine Lady

I

At death's door: how is it—
On the edge of that old mountain, looking out
Through windows of a darkened villa
On and on, far across Florence? Mist—
Insatiable and dull—
Hoods the ground, and those
Loved and clean-cut forms go shapeless,
Dim. Dear Lady,
Can we then help you move
Through realms of mist
By seeing you so clear,
Who greeted us erect and sure?

II

At death's door: how was it—
From the final edge of suffering, looking back
On all the sunlight, terraced years,
Back and back, far across Europe? Death—
Insatiable and cruel—
Stabbed the air, and those
Loved and clean-cut forms went shapeless,
Fell. Dear Lady,
Could we have helped you move
Through realms of dark
By seeing you so clear,
Who greeted us erect and sure?

25

City Afternoon

Far, far down
The earth rumbles in sleep;
Up through its iron grille,
The subway, black as a chimney-
Sweep, growls. An escalator rides
On dinosaur spines
Toward day. And on beyond,
Old bones, bottles,
A dismantled piano, sets
Of Mrs. Humphrey Ward all whirl
In the new disposal-unit; above
Its din, apartments are tenanted
Tight as hen-houses, people roosting
In every cupboard. Eight storeys
Up, pigeons nest on the noise
Or strut above it; higher,
The outcast sun serves its lean meat
Of light.

The whinnying
Of Venetian blinds has ceased: we sit
Invisible in this room,
Behind glass. In a lull,
A chance abatement of sound, a scalping
Silence, far
Down we hear the Iron
Maiden whisper,
Closing upon her spikes.

Portrait of the Boy as Artist

Were he composer, he would surely write
A quartet for three orchestras, one train:
After the penny-whistle's turn, he might —
With ten bull-fiddles purring the refrain —
Dub in a lion to outroar the night.

Were he a painter, he would loose such bolts
Of color as would scare the sun, abash
Rainbows: a palomino-coated colt
Gallops on every speckled plain: a gashed
Knee bleeds rubies: frogs are emerald.

Were he a poet with the gift of tongues,
He'd scale the Andes in a metaphor.
Race Theseus in the labyrinth, among
Larks and angels act as troubadour,
For Daniel Boone shout at the top of his lungs.

Clear-eyed he sallies forth upon the field,
Holding close to his ear the shell of the world.

Home Leave

With seven matching calfskin cases for his new suits—
Wife and three children following up the plank—
The Colonel shepherds his brood on board.

As the band pumps out "Arrivederci
Roma," the airman's apple
Face bobs over the first-class rail;
Across the watery gap, Sicilian
Crowds like lemmings rush at the narrowing pier.

Poised on the balls of his feet, the athlete
Goes below. Headwaiters
Screen him with menus; sommeliers
Approach on the double; corks pop to the creaking
Of timbers, while he dreams
Of winning every ship's pool.

Florid, the airman bunts
Favors around the dance floor: sky-blue-pink
Balloons doze on the air. It is the Captain's
Dinner; haloed in streamers, he romps
With a Duchess and wins
At Musical Chairs.

Later, on the boat-deck, laced
Tight as a hammock by Irish
Whiskey, the athlete nuzzles the nurse. Collapsed
Like a tent around her, he rolls
With the ship.

After breakfast, the children on deck, New York
Near, balling his fists, the hero
Turns on his wife:
He hits out as if to do her honor.

With seven matching calfskin cases for his new suits—
Wife and children following down the plank—
The Colonel shepherds his brood ashore.

In forest-green sportcoat and desert brogans, he passes
Through Customs like quicksilver. His wife
Is heavily veiled; her three
Children follow like figures in effigy.

Tramontana

Down from the north,
Clearing the hill's
Snow-topped shoulder,
Lashing the pale
Brittle grass,
The wind wheels.

Skimming the land
Low, like a sickle,
Shaking the trees
Barren that feel
Its vehement breath,
Taunting the bells'
Tranquil high
Calm as they peal
Notes like moons,
The wind growls
In mock singsong.

Arguing all
Day, all night
Plaguing, the dull
River of sound
Rises, fills
Our being, and mind
Taut as a sail
Snaps: in its
Continual bellow
We choke, drown;
The wind kills.

Sirocco

Wind? This is no wind
Jaunty or wild like the others—
A substance buffing the skin—

This is a toad's wind:
Cantankerous and dull,
Irresolute, our brains

Are waterlogged; we quarrel
Spitting out yellow dust,
Ugly as puffballs

In the mustard-colored day;
Slack as a toad, our bleached
Land shimmers under its brassy

Sky. Amphibian green,
The warm consumptive air
Lowers, and will not turn

Inside out to keen and blow!
Fruit rots upon the vine;
The heart may start to mildew,

Rage take us by the throat,
Blood scald the eye until,
Stifling, we fall apart

Down to a lesser world.
This wind that hates the mind
Squats on till all is soiled.

Mistral

Percussive, furious, this wind
Sweeps down the mountain, and
Under its pennon of skirling air
Blows through each red-tiled house as if
Nothing were there: Mistral,
Quartz-clear, spread-eagle,
Falls on the sea.
Gust upon gust batters
The surface—darkening blue—
Into a thousand scalloped fans. Where
Shall our noontime friends,
Cicada, hummingbird,
Who stitched the air with sound and speed,
Now hide? All rocks, islands, peninsulas
Draw near, hitch up their chairs,
Companions in this clearer, clean
Air, while inland fields are stripped of soil.
As I start home, a coven
Of winds is let loose at every corner;
Alone in a howling
Waste, figurehead sculptured in air,
Bent low, deafened, I plunge
On, blind in the eye of the storm.

Ballade of the Inventory: In Provence

Crying havoc through its recumbent
Oval mouth, the chandelier
Is, from below, a virulent
Iron mask; to one less near,
Indifferent, it becomes a mere
Distasteful fixture, number nine
Marked on the inventory here,
While the wind harries the great pine.

Item: one terrace with cement
Flooring, a locked armoire, five clear
Panes—*en guillotine*— a bent
Brass curtain rod, nine rings, a fear
Of things unlisted, a chiffonier
That teeters; two sponge-racks, one tine
Missing; all form a lavaliere—
While the wind harries the great pine—

Or silken noose. What treasure spent,
What pride of possession, on this gear
Dusty, dimmed, impermanent,
Provisional. When nothing's dear
To anyone alive, a queer
Mélange remains. The sweet woodbine
Flaunts from a wall its green revere,
While the wind harries the great pine.

Etched poet of Provence, veneer
Peeling from your frame, we drink this wine
To do you honor. Could you but hear,
While the wind harries the great pine!

In Autumn

Redmen come
Lounging in pale sedans and
Then, at some entrance to the wilderness,
Dismount. Storming
Hill after hill,
Redcoated irregulars march,
Holding their guns like flagpoles;
Flannel men, pocketing small game,
Stamp through our threadbare wood . . .

Then head for home,
Guns at half-mast
For the carcass roped to the hood
Of the pale sedan.
Horns hook out over a headlight,
Nostrils drip
Blood on the fender, eyeballs bulge
At death. The male emblem is red.
Does that car not bear
Sorry insignia: brown,
On a field of pastel,
A stag dormant, antlered?

The Gallery

Into an empty cube
We step: the gallery,
Hung with ivory walls, lies still
As a squash court foundered in depths of sea.
Like players entering, we stare
Above the horizon line to where
Each opulent canvas, back to wall,
Confronts the room.
                    And then gaze on till sight
Flickers, and vision swims
In an emulsion of color, till down
Their cones of intervening air
The chipped-glass fragments form and blur.
Paintings upon four walls—nothing alive
But painting. When we have gone,
Pictures in their magnificence remain,
Tranquil as spring looking in at an open window
On an empty room.

Death of a Vermont Farm Woman

Is it time now to go away?
July is nearly over; hay
Fattens the barn, the herds are strong,
Our old fields prosper; these long
Green evenings will keep death at bay.

Last winter lingered; it was May
Before a flowering lilac spray
Barred cold for ever. I was wrong.
                    Is it time now?

Six decades vanished in a day!
I bore four sons: one lives; they
Were all good men; three dying young
Was hard on us. I have looked long
For these hills to show me where peace lay . . .
                    Is it time now?

L'Ile du Levant: The Nudist Colony

All the wide air was trawled for cloud
And then that mass confined in a grey net
And moored to the horizon. Bowed

Down, the golden island under
A dull sky was not at its best; its heyday
Is when the heat crackles, the sun

Pours like a boiling waterfall
On matted underbrush and thicket, on
Boulder, dust; and, over all,

Cicadas at their pastime, drilling
Eyelets of sound, so many midget Singer
Sewing machines: busy, then still.

Landing beyond a thorny curve
We climbed down to the colony, extended
On its plot of beach. In the sudden swerve

Of every eye, they saw as one,
These Nudists on vacation, half their days
Prone, determined as chameleons

To match the ground beneath. At ease
Within a sandy cage, they turned to stare
Up at us clad identities

Who came to stare as openly
As if we too had railings fore and back
And the whole mind of a menagerie.

Such freedom of the flesh, if brave,
Lacks subtlety: a coat of sunburn can
Be badly cut. Well-tailored love

Not only demonstrates but hides,
Not only lodges with variety
But will keep private its dark bed.

We rose: below us golden-brown
Bodies of young and old, heavy and lean,
Lay beached upon the afternoon.

While water, casual as skin,
Bore our departing boat, we saw a form
In relief against the rocky line

And stood to wave farewell from our
World to his, even as charcoal dusk
Effaced his lazy semaphore.

The Triumphs

for
Milton Saul

The Triumph of Time

      ... Mounted on its triumphal chariot, Earth,
Shawled with the changing seasons, casts them off
In execution of a solemn dance:

Valleys the snow has leveled sink with spring
And hills start upward on a wave of green,
Warm winds sweep down on fallow pastures ... How
Easily summer conquers: liberal,
It broods upon the world as a trapeze
Hangs poised above its long trajectory.
Autumn: a crazy hunter comes to poach
Inflaming all upon a zigzag path
Magenta, tangerine — the woods are torn
Asunder. Soon an old man whose mackintosh
Flaps about narrow flanks, will quit the house
And, hourglass in hand, check the sundial.
Old Doge, old Cupid, the sun at your time of year
Is pale as death; — and is it death that comes,
Darkening the wind?
      Although the dance would seem
To have reached its end, still clockwise earth will swing,
In each triumphant season witnessing
How this, this temporal dance, breaks from eternal
     love. ...

The Triumph of Chastity

Over the plain two dark
Equestrian figures pound
Charging full tilt at spring;
Behind them burnt-over ground,
A desolate panel stretches,
A long dun scarf unwound.

The taller, Cavalier
Hatred, his horny gut
Wild with the heat of their ride
Spurs onward, faster yet
Must he race his mighty Arab
Stallion; upon her jennet

Side-saddle, stride for stride,
Gallops the Lady, fleet
Ambition; her sallow hair
Streams on the wind like light,
Cold as a cameo
Her face. They sow a great

Swathe of the plain with dust;
On, on he presses. Now,
Mantles like bellying sails,
They scud at the wood, and so
Storm forward till he reins in, —
Midnight upon his brow,

Caparisoned in jet,
Harness, panache of black
Spume-flecked, his stallion's eye
Encrimsoned; — they rein back
To their haunches the quivering steeds
At the brink: — Scrub, tamarack,

Meadows defoliate,
Autumnal. They who have
Outrun the spring, now halt
To seek as in a cheval-
Glass one eternal face.
Each stares at his own self-love.

The Triumph of Love

As from some grand
Venetian ballroom ceiling
Veronese's cupids
Gaze
Down, ringed
About the cupola,
Coronas of bright hair
Encircling them with light, suspended
There, clipped sturdy wings
Folded, chin in hand
Or holding tight the attic balcony which like
The top rung of a ladder wells
Dizzily above us who look up,
Heads thrown back, craning, seeking our
Reflected stare:

So toward the sleeping child do we
Converge,
Eyelids lowered and look down,
Once more so moved that all
Space dwindles
And the Palace walls
Are scaled to inches by our deepening love.

The Triumph of Death

Illusion forms before us like a grove
Of aspen hazing all the summer air
As we approach a new plateau of love.

With discs of light and shade, vibration of
Leaf-candelabra, dim, all-tremulous there,
Illusion forms before us like a grove

And bends in welcome: with each step we move
Nearer, quick with desire, quick to dare.
As we approach a new plateau of love,

New passion, new adventure wait above
And call to our drumming blood; all unaware
Illusion forms before us like a grove

In a mirage, we reach out to take Love
In our arms, compelled by one another's stare.
As we approach a new plateau of love

The aspen sigh in mockery: then have
We come this way before? Staining the air,
Illusion forms before us like a grove
As we approach a new plateau of love.

The Triumph of Pride

Not to retain,
Not to let go;
Not to approve—

Even of the blue heron
That soars and is gone—
Of anyone

Giving pleasure or pain—
Flown away so
Quickly, like love.

The Triumph of Truth

Speaking out of a clear sky
I greeted two people at once; perhaps my eye
Saw less the real than the imagined figure.
These two repassed, rhythmically, like a fan,
Or like two dancers swaying
Apart, then eclipsing the other.

In an old painting Truth is drawn
In triumph by two elephants: a woman
Holding a great sword and a golden book,
While all around her, kings, philosophers,
And poets in her train
Nod and debate again.

How the rude sun has bronzed their skin!
See how her jeweled book reflects the inner
Light of their noble faces, of their crowns.
Truth's jet-black broadsword shudders over all,
An iron ruler poised,
That suddenly may sweep down.

Out of a clear sky Art speaks
The truth; two dancers separate and mix;
Each of us is an atoll whose protective
Shell is hard. But, a true mariner,
Art looks far out, and Truth
In triumph rides, with Love.

In the Cold Country

━━❯❮❯❮━━

for
Ximena de Angulo

Primavera

The horse with consumption coughed like the end
     of the world.
We heard its tremblors echo in that dry bark,
But on our carriage rolled; we minted miles,
Like hoops our coined wheels rolled until the dark
Came down upon the city, and grey shade
Merged all the cathedral's zebra stripes; the park
Recessed for night, vendors' flags, bird-wings furled.

Onward and on we rode until the dawn.
From jeweled opera-box and catacomb
We summoned up the past: released, the ghosts
Came forth in cloth of gold and tilting heaume
In every city street and horned lane
Whose flowers pell-mell hung down, geranium foam
From walls all staunch with red, red staunched by stone.

And on and on; where would the journey end?
Giotto conceived a tower in pure air,
Heraldic rainbow; balanced on her shell
All beauty woke in Aphrodite fair
As history's fairest. Now to trespassers
On the volcano's flank the tocsins blare:
Our mare's obsidian hooves foreknelled the end.

Portrait of an Artist

For dear life some do
Many a hard thing,
Train the meticulous mind
Upon meaning, seek
And find, and yet discard
All that is not of reality's tough rind.

A cool divining rod,
The heart, another tool,
Keen as a hawk's eye,
Supple as water, bends
Responsive to all four
Humors. In many sympathy runs dry

Or blots and blurs. To be
Ascetic for life's sake,
Honest and passionate,
Is rare. I think of those
Images of Buddha placed
In shells, and later found encased in pearl.

Light and Dark

Lady, take care; for in the diamond eyes
Of old old men is figured your undoing;
Love is turned in behind the wrinkled lids
To nurse their fear and scorn at their near going.
Flesh hangs like the curtains in a house
Long unused, damp as cellars without wine;
They are the future of us all, when we
Will be dried-leaf-thin, the sour whine
Of a siren's diminuendo. They have no past
But egg-husks shattered to a rubbish heap
By memory's looting. Do not follow them
To their camp pitched in a cranny, do not keep
To the road for them, a weary weary yard
Will bring you in; that beckoning host ahead,
Inn-keeper Death, has but to lift his hat
To topple the oldster in the dust. Read,
Poor old man, the sensual moral; sleep
Narrow in your bed, wear no
More so bright a rose in your lapel;
The spell of the world is loosed, it is time to go.

The Heart of Europe

See the crazy gate
Or crazy house atilt, terraced with air
Where solid wall once stood, cliff-dwellers' home.
Or here a man,
A soldier once, night-watching out the day,
Life's blinders are put on him young.
He sells
Pencils, we turn away; the penny price
Is too great for this sideshow of a world;
Pity, a flea-bite, fades.
A witch's brew
May have reduced all to a crazy-quilt,
A patchwork satire on the grace of man,
So limber in the grace of God
He, mountebank animal, makes his cities silt
Overnight. The eye of newt, bull's ear,
Blood of an infant born within wedlock,
Alchemy's golden key, the soldiers' cube
Of sustenance, all these have wreaked a spell
Every old woman mumbles endlessly.
Whether we brood or work or sit
Vacant and staring, how the cold March winds
Blow through the defenceless houses, over the limp
Flags of laundry hung from the ruins,
Upon the helpless old, for all are old,
Freezing them in its icy tourniquet.
But yet throughout, hate grows, builds up to tower
A flaming Lucifer higher than the spires
Of the dark drugged cathedrals;
He bends down
In triumph over the wreckage of the town.

Everywoman

Oh where are you riding, lady,
So fast on your mindless horse?
What wonder has set the compass
That leads you this skyline course;
What goal or what comfort, lady,
Call with such force?

Oh where are you riding, riding?
For autumn burns in the eyes
Of those you pass so gaily
In your fresh greening guise;
The leaves have sickened, lady,
And their sap dries.

Oh where, oh where are you riding?
Your horse is a hollow gong
Whose hoofbeats fade to an echo
As thin as your wisp of song;
No flesh to your grasp, none, lady,
And the nights grow long.

The Stag of God

The neck of the white stag of the valley
Yearns toward the sky with such grace
That his soul can but continue this aspiration
Further in space;

Firm-moulded spire of ivory
Stretched up, up, as if to touch
The tenderest spiced leaves in Eden.
No distrust

Deepens the shadow of his eyes
Or sets the muscles of his sturdy shoulders
Jangling. The cool powerful basilica
Of his body holds

Firm in the agony of spring
And in the passion of the storm,
White and firm after all the years that crept
By his white form.

Yet the bleached stag of the valley
Has no shadow to cast upon the earth
To warm it, no full-throated gospel-call
To reach every hearth;

His mighty haunches hold but do not spring
Forward and outward in sympathy
Or penance; were he ever to regain
Sinew and elasticity

He might not, high and cold upon the land
Outworn as the poor Ark on Ararat,
Look useless down while the tormented world
Seeks past that spot.

Landscape and Figure

The concrete-colored sky
Loomed sullen overhead
As I, at the highway edge,
Scuffed out my private track
In the shale of the road's shoulder.
Each auto, a torpedo,
Sped through its tube of air;
I ran, but they fled past me
As if I were standing still,
Immobile as a scarecrow
Upon whose battered hat
All seasons, weathers fall.
These were two worlds, and speed
Was killer king; I feared
Each one might end my walking.

How strange the sleight-of-hand
Of memory, that I should
Recall, at such a time,
This Mughal painting: when
On Shah Jehan its curious
Shadow fell, must he
Not have rejoiced to feel
Marked by its beauty in
Intaglio? Here reigns
Color, landscape, form,
Rock, peacock, antelope
Composed on an emerald field;
While at the plane-tree's trunk
See how the tawny hunter
Barefoot mounts swift, the sky
Of golden light aglow
All about the ecstatic tree.

Emblazoned, embossed with green,
Scarlet and tourmaline,
Topaz, or leaves of brass,
It stands. The squirrel-prey,
Intent, bead-sharp their eyes,
Flirt dangerward their tails,
Then feint, like acrobats,
In tawny rivulets,
Flash deeper, to flash away
Behind the pendent leaves.

Color, color. Oh,
Was this picture dead in the real
Arterial vista, or was
This roadway a mirage,
A trick of vision? There
Lay only the cold March day,
The narrowing tarmac tape
And the saurian machines,
Whose deaf-mute drivers sat
Remote in their diamond aim,
As if they would run right out
Of time. The leaden street
Mirrored the sky; in fear
I turned back for my car.

The New Leda

Goosegirl, your feet are slow
And heavy with acceptance, while the echo
Of what will come
Gathers momentum and batters at your eardrum.

The future hangs
Over you like an airborne bell, its clangs
Will gut your heart, will keep
Up their reverberant assault, no sleep

Will be the same again;
Marked, muted by this inexorable hyphen
You cannot be the same;
There is no sanctuary, the god will come

And bed you in his plumage;
Intent, bird-lidded, knotted in his rage
Of lust he will flail down
Every abject appeal. . . . Quiet in gown

Of white the bride of Christ
Moves down the waiting nave as if her wrist
Were held and she led,
Hands heart obeying the seeing unseen Dead,

And she led on as though
Walking through shallow water, where the slow
Tide urges at her feet
But checks their driftwood longing. Will the sweet

Wan dedicated face,
Inward as some old painting, find a place
Of sweetest rest, a home
Now in the Spirit's mansion and catacomb?

Will she encounter love,
Laughter, pain and grief, or will she live
For centuries encased
In waterglass serenity; the taste

Of an eternal death
In life upon her lips, although breath
Cannot fail? Her
Limbo holds her like a fly in amber,

Beyond the reach of life.
Sisters, wastrels, when will you have enough
Of sacrifice and harm
And deprivation? Remember the mighty arm

That, white and sick with strain,
Wrestled the whole night out until the plain
Was light and he could see
Deep down the precipice of self, his adversary

And ask his blessing. Either
Make peace with yourselves, or live locked in such war
As, ruinous from the start,
Turns dark with pity Jacob's brazen heart.

Coq de Combat

There Jack-cock struts
Rattling his brassy plumage,
Gamey torso rearing,
Aims his beak
And then,
Oh-ho, lets loose a challenge
That, like darts,
Will smite the target ear,—
Coco-rico!

How can this cocky mobster know
That soon the tumbrils of the night
Will move to harvest darkness,
Or the stars
Like crocuses will close;
The Cyclops moon
All day must be put out,
Its eye interred
In a great vault blue as forget-me-not?

Our brave cock struts:
This very day
May be his day for battle
When, armed cap-à-pie,
All rapier beak and spurs,
Angry, leaping, he'll try
To blood-let and life-let his enemy.
Coco-rico!

Now he,
A feathered timepiece,
Monitor of dawn,
At this gargantuan ring presides,
In his turn bells us out
To do, endure, or die,—
Coco-rico!

In a Prospect of Flowers

OF A PAINTER DROWNED IN HIS TWENTIETH YEAR

As in his tomb
In amethystine water the artist lies,
Framed by raw cement, lapped
By many-petalled sunlight
That engraves
Each phosphorent particle.

He
Hangs there face down,
His body ominous in this design,
Dark head resting on the lapis-lazuli
Empty bosom of water,
Flung
Like Icarus.
Now no vision can again
Furnish those hands with vision
Or
That heart with color.

Royal palms,
The columns of some ancient portico,
Incline;
And we, downcast
At this imagined brink,
Lament and praise—
Within a fatal aquarelle—
The lineaments of the ideal.

Mirror Image: Port-au-Prince

Au petit
Salon de Coiffeur,
Monique's / hands fork
like lightning, like a baton
rise / to lead her client's hair
in *repassage:* she irons out the kinks.
Madame's brown cheek / is dusted over with a
paler shade / of costly powder. Nails and lips are red.

Her matching lips and nails incarnadined, / in the
next booth Madam consults her face / imprisoned
in the glass. Her lovely tan / is almost
gone. Oh, watch Yvonne's astute /
conductor fingers set the
permanent, / *In little*
Drawing-room of
Hairdresser!

Relatives

Their eyes go out on stalks like crabs' to the closet;
Sipping their tea they uncoil a précis,
Rumours of shame, malfeasance, bizarre ills
Among the invisible family choir. They covet
Each out-turned glance, all hawsers loaned to land
As I move slowly waterward; they shock
And simper, crouching ringed upon the deck
Rattling the bony dice of tribal fate.
It is time, you jackanapes crew! The moon lets down
The shelled gold of her wake on the river ahead.
It is time to unpilot you; we shall not be late.

The Nuns Assist at Childbirth

Robed in dungeon black, in mourning
For themselves they pass, repace
The dark linoleum corridors
Of humid wards, sure in the grace

Of self-denial. Blown by duty,
Jet sails borne by a high wind,
Only the face and hands creep through
The shapeless clothing, to remind

One that a woman lives within
The wrappings of this strange cocoon.
Her hands reach from these veils of death
To harvest a child from the raw womb.

The metal scales of paradox
Tip here then there. What can the nun
Think of the butchery of birth,
Mastery of the flesh, this one

Vigorous mystery? Rude life
From the volcano rolls and pours,
Tragic, regenerate, wild. Sad
The unborn wait behind closed doors.

Morning-Glory

FOR C.W.

Now when spiralling summer burns
Its way toward autumn, on this vine
The morning-glory opens such
Buoyant parasols of blue,
Uplifted into light, as to
Recover spring . . . recovering much
More: the azure of a mind
And cloudless heart to which we turn.

In the Cold Country

We came so trustingly, for love, but these
Lowlands, flatlands, near beneath the sea
Point with their cautionary bones of sand
To exorcize, submerge us; we stay free
Only as mermaids glittering in the waves:
Mermaids of the imagination, young
A spring ago, who know our loveliness
Banished, like fireflies at winter's breath,
Because none saw; these vines about our necks
We placed in welcome once, but now as wreath
Against the scalpel cold; still cold creeps in
To grow like ivy over our chilling bodies
Into our blood. Now in our diamond dress
We wive only the sequins of the sea.
The lowlands have rejected us. They lie
Athwart the whispering waters like a scar
On a mirage of glass; the dooming land,
Where nothing can take root but frost, has won.
And what of warmth and what of joy? They are
Sequestered elsewhere, southward, where the sun
Speaks. For all our mermaid vigilance
And balance, all goes under; underneath
The land's grey wave we falter and fall back
To hibernate within the caves of death.

Views of the Oxford Colleges

Oxford abounds in fern and bird-watcher.
It is a lovely place when its short spring
Softens the chilblained air, and coats the stone
Tombs of buildings with its early green.
It is most lovely to the mind's eye
When age and earnestness discreetly sing.

Prudence and earnestness discreetly sing
Their muted canticles; the eighty odd
Year old, the old at twenty-five, or the
Intelligent wrapped in long mufflers nod
At beauty passing, but their baths are cold,
They have an ague and believe in God.

The ague holds, and the belief in God
Carries them through the valley of depression,
Bleak as any mine, like Cromwell who,
Roundheaded in his obstinacy, rang down
A curtain on felicity; the past
Is moored in Oxford firm as an obsession.

Moored in Oxford firm as an obession,
Man opens his umbrella which will turn
Back the sensual sun; he cannot feel —
Poor dampened Adam — love or beauty burn
Caught within the spokes of that black wheel.
Oxford abounds in bird-watcher and fern.

The Don

A cockney rounds the corner, laundry pins
Upon his nose; a deathshead spouting Greek
Totters abaft the podium: dates of birth
And death sicken the air like blackboard chalk.
The words are mouthed and mumbled till they fall,
Shredded, behind his hand, in the long hall.
This is the scholiast's black mass; we sit
And fret to see each poem impaled, dead
As butterfly on pin, as dried egg-shell.
Necromancer of learning, a black bat
With wing extended over literature,
He sweeps to rend Adonis' living body.
Beauty is extinguished, value gone;
Silence in the hall; dark in the hall; all's done.

Indian Summer

This man, this stranger in my arms
Lies quiet now, below in sleep,
Lost in the deep seine of his dream.
How wide the net is cast, far out, far down,
But his dream plumbs himself; mine is my own.

Two feral figures in the jungle half-
Light taut in struggle
Shoulder to shoulder,
Cold hate, colder force
In the leashed clash of wrestlers
Clasped in war in
One another's arms;
There they enact
The ancient drama of possession.
But who has won?
Deep down within the womb
Of dream, of his own dream,
Each acts his part, and is by it possessed.

Time's horn of plenty spills
Out to us her dialectic
Changing forms;
No one can say
When love will take root,
Run wildfire up the heart's trellis. We
Harbor such diversity
That turning now we find
The future in our arms,
A golden cataract that comes
Out of the cornucopia of dream.

Lament

Often thinking of death one dreams of a river
Whose sensual waters, black as pitchblende, roll
Out as if powered, poured by some huge engine.
Light grazes the water, refracts; its depths are too old
For eye or for light to pierce. But death, the sure diver,

Cuts rapier-quick his element, and casts
Down all that his traveling touched. The waterlogged
Dead stuff of branch or animal floats by,
Insects skim, a visored turtle flogs
Its way along, eddies drink air and are lost.

We who stand on the bank in the luminous quiet
Of evening, our hands linked, sorrowing, face
The wilderness that waits beyond the river.
The wild cannot rest with the tame, the forest preys
Always upon its own to prey, and not

Till death come cradle them will they pause for peace.
We have read justice on what cannot change,
On nature pitched too high for harmony,
And so were right and wrong. And so the strange
Wild frantic clear-eyed ones are gone. Released

From their war with life now, on the breast of the river
We see them pass, and half the world is dressed
In sunlight's full regalia, while thunders rear
And clang their giant tympani; the west
Awaits its sun at the end of the impenetrable river.

The Critic

Ugolino takes his rest,
For rest he needs after such labor;
He has prepared a tasty stew
Neglecting neither sauce nor savor;
His spiritual fathers he has cooked,
Basted, spitted and sprigged with bay,
His cultural fathers he has eaten,
And now he's quite as great as they.
Great with father sitteth he
Happy, for they are no more:
Eliot, with thyme bedight,
Tossed like Leander to the shore;
Yeats tumbled to oblivion
Without a mourner; Ugolino
Surveys his future dancing bright
As Theda Bara at the Kino.
He wears contentment like a wreath
And for a smile an orange rind,
There is no art but in his belch
Whose stomach's bigger than his mind.

The Bar at the Carrousel

Cloche-hatted like Hermes, game-feathered for wings,
Emotion drives her body as one leans
Against the storm-swept tiller, features sharp
With rage and sting.

She sits there, perches, while her love, her friend,
Placed doll-like between her and the man
Revolves in coquetry, the prey of each,
Who both intend

That she shall wear their colors, turning now
To the distraught rouged mask, then to the man's
Jowled face, his eyes like pegs, but free in the world
To come or go.

The rioting heart of Sappho's stormy daughter
Sends out hate which even he can feel
Who takes his leave abruptly, caring little;
The usual slur

Of the world falls off like spray from a plunging bow.
She aches with triumph, and the muscles round
Her thin lips swell with power, a pretty death-
Mask quickening now.

In this museum, the world, we have a fine
Prospect of ancient gods, nor should we fail
To recognize here Hermes as death's agent.
The androgyne

At home in her half-world, woman's companion,
Seneschal among the shadows, waits
To guide her curving way until she wanders
All compass gone.

The Balcony

Light playing on the water plays on the trees,
Shimmers and scatters, dowering them with light.
All things partake of the sun's strength,
The long warm hand of heaven is on us until night.

As from a prow that juts in space we watch
Stipple of wind upon the quiet lake,
Each idle insect droning on,
And high above our heads see heron in echelon

Ferry across on deep unhurried wing.
All these foreshortened forms your eyes compose
And render to my understanding
So that the sunlight too reflects your influence.

Such wisdom near me, I am nearer the light
Whose every incident you so endow.
This is immediacy, this is love;
And by its gracious hand I wake from darkest night.

The Undersea Farmer

To dream of islands . . .
The mind's eye moves and planes
Up the incline of sea,
They lie atilt there
Against the horizon. Islands

Are moored on shoals
And tower above the vaults
Of black water, pyramids
Of depth, where old
Benumbed seas chill the shoals;

What arteries
Of light shaft down these fathoms
At length snuff out in black,
The sea-pit water
Muffles even the arteries

Of the imagination
But as it muffles, fills.
Our tines touch depth and surface
As we roll
In our imagination,

In the sea,
In the glaucous sunny deep water
Between worlds. A shark
That goes his easy
Narrative through our sea,

Poses a model
Gesture in his here-
To-there progress, long
Curving pentameter
Of skaters; or note a model

Of the oblique in the flying
Fish's brushing shadow
While he high-tails it over
The waves; he grazes
Us only with his dark flying-

Away symbol
For our notebooks and hope and joy;
If we prefer the conceptual
Seahorse, he rides
The waves as if a symbol

Of inwardness mounted
There; flesh tucked beneath
His bony plates; all outline,
But motored
From within; my mounting

Wonder at such
Proliferation allows
But a glimpse at the shagreen
Sea urchin, delicate
As Christmas tree ornaments, such

Mystery in
Its being, one can only
Believe that it does breathe.
These denizens
Of form are catalysts in

Our minds; so let us go
Hand over hand back toward
The watery skylight, toward land,
Afraid only of letting
Our subaqueous lifeline go.

Annunciation

Time, a recording angel, bends
One knee upon the grass:
There in the azure close of day
Remote against the arras
Of herb and floweret he broods
On what may come to pass.

Shadows of afternoon arrange
A cloak about her head;
Silent she stands beneath the groined
Portal, awaiting word
Or sign from that ghostly visitor
Of what will be her meed:

Will he say nothing, and she turn
Her back and go within?
Or, waxing, in a little while
Step out upon a scene
Of Tuscan summer, bearing proud
Contour of mandolin?

On a Bougainvillæa Vine
at the Summer Palace

Under the sovereign crests of dead volcanoes,
See how the lizards move in courtly play;
How when the regnant male
Fills the loose bagpipe of his throat with air,
His mate will scale
Some vine portcullis, quiver, halt, then peer—
Eyes sharp as pins—
At that grandee posed stiff with self-esteem,
His twiglike tail acurve.

What palaces lie hid in vines! She sees
Chameleon greenrooms opening on such
Elite boudoirs,
Flowers as bright as massacres; should she
Not try their spiring tendrils
That like string
Hammocks are slung upon the open air?
Tensing his tiny jaw, he seems to smile;
And while all nature sways,
Lightly rides his delicate trapeze.

A virid arrow parts
The leaves—she's at
His side. Then darts away; he following,
They lose themselves within the redolent shade. . . .
Quiet the palace lies
Under the sun's green thumb,
As if marauding winter would never come.

The Homecoming

All the great voyagers return
Homeward as on an arc of thought;
Home like a ruby beacon burns
As they crest wind, scale wave, soar air;
All the great voyagers return,

Though we who wait never have done
Fearing the piteous accidents,
The coral reef sharp as the bones
It has betrayed, fate's cormorant
Unleashed, whose diving's never done.

Even the voyager of mind
May fail beneath behemoth's weight;
Oh, the world's bawdy carcass blinds
All but the boldest, rots the sails
And swamps the voyaging of the mind.

But all the great voyagers return
Home like the hunter, like the hare
To its burrow; below, earth's axle turns
To speed their coming, the following fair
Winds bless their voyage, blow their safe return.

from
Looking up at Leaves

In Memory
Harriott Allen

There was always this groundswell of love —
Now — a wave on the beach — it is all over:
There is no message left upon the sand.
Mother-of-pearl worn hollow, I bend
To listen for that greygreen groundswell.

for
Charlee and Dick Wilbur

A Short Way by Air

Out Fishing

We went out, early one morning,
Over the loud marches of the sea,
In our walnut-shell boat,
Tip-tilting over that blue vacancy.

Combering, coming in,
The waves shellacked us, left us breathless, ill;
Hour on hour, out
Of this emptiness no fish rose, until

The great one struck that twine-
Wrapped flying-fish hard, turned and bolted
Off through the swelling sea
By a twist of his shoulder, with me tied fast; my rod

Held him, his hook held me,
In tug-of-war — sidesaddle on the ocean
I rode out the flaring waves,
Rode till the great fish sounded; by his submersion

He snapped the line, we lost
All contact, north, south, west, my adversary
Storms on through his world
Of water: I do not know him: he does not know me.

Dead Toucan: Guadeloupe

Down like the oval fall of a hammer
The great bill went,
Trailed by its feather-duster body
Splat on cement.
His mates fell out of countenance,
All listened, shivering in the sun,
For what was off, amiss:
In his pretend haven under a flame tree
The agouti crouched, chewed on his spittle, shook,
The porcupine rolled in his box, the parakeets
Chattered regrets,
Knowing something was wrong in their hot Eden:
That their King had followed his heavy fate to earth;
And his superb
Accomplishment,
His miracle of balance,
Had come to nothing, nothing. . . .
A beak with a panache
Chucked like an old shell back to the Caribbean.

Troy Weight Taken

We do not need to comb
Arkansas to find
Rubies; loneliness
Vanishes in this crystal-
Clear actual air,
And one by one makes one.
Love tempers us, and every
True embrace is carved
In ivory; lasts; although
My eyes are shut, I learn
Each golden day that golden
Moorings hold me home.

A Letter from the Caribbean

Breezeways in the tropics winnow the air,
Are ajar to its least breath
But hold back, in a feint of architecture,
The boisterous sun
Pouring down upon

The island like a cloudburst. They
Slant to loft air, they curve, they screen
The wind's wild gaiety
Which tosses palm
Branches about like a marshal's plumes.

Within this filtered, latticed
World, where spools of shadow
Form, lift and change,
The triumph of incoming air
Is that it is there,

Cooling and salving us. Louvers,
Trellises, vines—music also—
Shape the arboreal wind, makes skeins
Of it, and a maze
To catch shade. The days

Are all variety, blowing;
Aswirl in a perpetual current
Of wind, shadow, sun,
I marvel at the capacity
Of memory

Which, in some deep pocket
Of my mind, preserves you whole—
As wind is wind, as the lion-taming
Sun is sun, you are, you stay:
Nothing is lost, nothing has blown away.

A Conversation

As we stood on the crushed stone
Of the drive, it was as if
A spring landscape unrolled
Between. Colors deep
As gems—the tapestry,
Intricate and rich,
Of a lifetime. I was
Assumed into this world;
These emblematic hues
Shone like vintage wine:
Jet—that contains darkness
For those who have known the worst;
Beige—parchment-colored,
On which a burning glass
Etches the mind's runes;
Turquoise—that mood of green
And blue, field and sky—
Blending, to stand out.
Artist and woman moved there
Each in her separate light,
Clear-cut against a silver
Background of dream—all
Colors blend in silver,
A molten gong—whose full
Resonance an artist
Brocades upon the soul.

On Galveston Beach

The sky was battened down
Low all around us. We stood up
Into a sea of air,
First comers to this Sicilian element,
Prospectors motionless in a bowl of blue.

Down-at-mouth at the rim,
The barely-breathing sea
Neighbored flat sand; it waited
As a pier does for some sightseer
Of horizons to wander out.

If the sky is indeed a bowl
Pressed over us by a huge hand,
We have fellow-creatures everywhere:
Sand in its patient minuteness,
That lean duck, his neck a hook, bobbing for fish,
Or those great mushrooms of the Gulf,
Jetsam jellyfish, in whose gills
Lie strands of aquamarine;
Their lives, so humpbacked and so white,
Resemble death. We stand awhile and watch
Waves worry them toward shore,
Before striking out in their sea.

Flight

One bails out into space
Each morning, distance

Is nothing: a subway stop,
A walk uphill. The Russian, well-equipped,

Trod space as though man had been twirling there
Always, a bauble on the chandelier

Of the firmament; attached by a beanie
Headdress, Leonov was fully

Aware that should the cord break
It would take

No time for him to die: or go
On into limbo,

A man-made satellite. . . . But he was
Under the proud eye of the world, unlike Goya's

Madman circling Toledo
Like a Barnum and Bailey missile

With no intent
Of destruction, lent

Terror only from his own terror,
Who rode the air

Hellbent, though no one thought to look up. . . .
A boy stepped

Into one car
Not the next, one segment of the river

Of the subway, and entered upon his death
As much by chance as by the icepick in his brain, the
wealth

Of his unlived good years
Spent in a moment; all our fear

Of the unknown, revulsion at brutality
Casts us out to the outer spaces of the mind, whence we

Will return only with time,
Realizing of him

That nothing is the same as one young man, one son,
One good bet, gone.

On Sleeping Together

Day becomes explicit. From this shared
Warmth we grew into together here in bed,
Concave as a hammock, we are all one piece
At the moment of waking: is that my arm, or this?
Still linked and folded, slowly we withdraw
Selves and bodies from our world of sleep.
Caught in silhouette, heroic figures
Dim in the toils of darkness, but now responding
To the bravura of conch-shell and drum,
Alive, we wake; waking, we separate,
With ceremony rise to greet the morning.

For Chloe

My cat kneads me with her rhythmic paws,
But this is in reverie, a work of affection;
She may see this warm base as a high table
Near which, below the salt, her mouse is et,
She wants thereafter her dark glade of purring
And a breathing body under her ribcase.

For Cleo

A different nature wanders through the door,
Brushing each corner in her satisfaction,
Curving by man, by furniture, well able
As any golden cat to charm and wait
Her golden due; she is; she warms a long slurring
Breath of congratulation, being at ease.

The Lace Maker

Needle, needle, open up
The convolvulus of your eye,
I must come upon it quick
Or my thread will die.

Night is settling down outside,
My sallow candle seems to thin,
But I must weave this laddered thread
To nest each rare space in.

It is dark. Darkness plaits a scarf
Over my eyes. Can finger sprout
Eyes at the tip to guide its work?
Each evening, I go out

To Sainte Gudule — if I can see
Needlepoint of aspiring stone,
The window's rose embroidery
Trained like a trumpet upon Heaven,

Then I may live; but if my sight
Narrows toward death, a black-avised
Gargoyle will jut out, grinning there,
Exulting in that swirling mist.

The Crane Chub — Barbados

Darling,
I learn
The full
Value
Of you
Again,
Savoring
The Crane
Chub
Who idles,
Mates,
And dies,
Near one
Single
Reef
Just off
St. Philip
Parish;
He loves
His own,
Is of
A flesh
So rare
He must
Be eaten
Just
Within
The hour.

As your
Absence
Goes so
Against
The tide—
Sun,
Love,
Wind—
I now
Partake
Of Crane
Chub:
And oh
His essence
Is
Less rare,
Bitter,
Within
The flaw
Of your
Not being
Here.

The Lovers of Delicate Things

IN MEMORIAM: WPD

William and I
     Always want too much —
Want people to be porcelain
     But also willing;
Want the sensitive brain
     To triumph over the doings

Of the rough outside world.
     William and I
Seem to be obdurate, only
     We melt at the ring
Of the wrong number, at the
     Wild hope that everything

Is about to work
     Out according to our notions.
William and I
     Balk, check rein
On the stampede of those ponies
     Within us, strike out from our pain

With sharp hooves.
     It is better to be lonely
Than wrong, we think, or tasteless.
     William and I,
By giving up, give less
     Of ourselves to be hurt. By

Self-effacement, that Puritan
    Mask, do we conceal
The structure of our pride.
    We should have turned,
William and I,
    Away from power, have learned

That control is not needed
    Over others; simply of oneself, for
The lover of delicate things
    Can reach out and destroy
That to which he most clings—
    William!—Not I!

Gulls

In their long
Arabesque, wings ferrying the steady
Cargo of the body,
Are strong

As mainsails;
Yet cutting into the sky they cut out paper-
Birds: themselves, shape;
They sickle

All that's in view,
Outrunning the westering tide in the face of the west
Wind, across distance —
m to *w* — *m* to *w* .

Footnote

Love is a great leveler.
Some of us
May fancy we have mastered desire—
Not likely; it's too imperious. For many
Love is a great
Barrier; some are ill
With fear of it. Few, really,
Have ever breathed its blue oracular air
Deep in their lungs. Love is a bell
That sounds and bodies forth the whole being.
We need own
So little: half a bed;
So much: hope that love is, will be
Love.

A Stand of Birches

FOR R.W.

Tall as if standing on jointed stilts,
This upright scaffolding,
These delicate laths
Firm to an altitude,
Much as 7-league boots might change
The gangling third son of all fairy-tale
To one fit to win The Princess.

There is something in this silhouette
Of courtier and hobbledehoy,
Opposites strung like wire over the high
Paneling of the shoulders: impatient, cool;
A laconic herald;
Pan in an Ascot tie.

There is a gardener, too, stubborn, yare,
Whose work terraces the hillsides
Of language, possessed
By a nomad cast of mind that ranges
Furlongs over a landscape
Of solitude and distance.

Something that Holbein would have paused
Over informs this face:
He might have seen—
Painted on wood—the clean
Jaw and square brow, caught in those shadowed eyes
Vision that brought cathedrals higher, higher,
Lofty as there was stone for them;
All lit, all colored by
A heaviness of light,
New England Gothic chiaroscuro.

So, like a stand of birches, be briary, bend,
Touch earth, whip back to your high stance again.

Dream of a Good Day

I dream of going in my outrigger canoe—
Buoyant, in balance upon each cobalt wave—
To follow the porpoise at his crescent play.

Or in my schooner, at its easy riding,
To imagine high in the crow's-nest—which the ship
Sedately nods this way and that— a bed
Of crimson peonies, mine for the conceiving.

After, to wander alone the high wind-lanes,
With language all one's passion: its topsail
Scudding—then made fast: the poem strengthening,
Quieting down. . . . A day to dream of—
Then in the colloquial evening to come back to love.

Sea School

This afternoon I swam with a school of fish.
Waiting in shallow water for the tide to change,
They swept at leisure through their green pleasance
Turning at will as one, or at some private
Signal all felt:
White and delicate, each one bedizened
By an ochre spot behind his sickle of gill,
Pale translucent fish they were, divided
By the hair-thin moustache-line of backbone.

We plied our way along, taking our ease,
In concert, as a school
Feeling the flickering lozenges of light,
Chickenwire of sunlight grazing us
As we passed up and down under its stroke.
So for an hour, an age, I swam with them,
One with the rhythm of the sea, weightless,
Graceful and casual in our schoolhood,
Within our coop of light,
One with a peace that might go on forever. . . .
Till, of a sudden, quick as a falling net,
Some thought embraced them: I watched them go
Tidily over the reef where I could not follow.

My Dear, Listen:

If what may be
Is to turn—by grace, by craft, into poetry,
Is it not fine
That there are ten
Or more varieties
Of wild cherry,
And as for maples
There are multiple
Sorts that range
All over our ancient
American topsoil?
But then all
Of these fair trees
Know what species
They are—to what greatness
They may rise:
Reaching toward that
Preordained height
Their nature allows
And their fortune hallows.
Increasing, sowing
Seedpods and catkins
That a future forest
Of individualists
Will be assured.
In this mulligan world
Such family strictness
And integrity is
Profoundly moving;

More than other beings
An artist should keep
The pathway open
To his inward life,
To that native self
That must daily be fed,
Pondered and watered
If what might be
Is to turn—by grace, by craft—into poetry.

For Katherine Anne Porter

MAY 15th, 1965

Madam, a siege
  Of heron
    Salutes you!

A spring of teal
  Flies criss-cross
    Through golden

Runnels of air, to say
  Luck, good omens!
    While a muster of peacock

Shows all-out
  Best wishes, a flight
    Of doves sends love;

A murmuration of starlings
  Builds up its iridescent
    Agreement

In trees, over fields; and then
  A watch of nightingales
    Flies in to do honor,—

And flies in through this fine
  Evening, to grace what all feel:
    An exaltation of larks!

Ode to Poseidon

LINES ON A GRECIAN URN RECENTLY ACQUIRED
BY THE WILLIAMS COLLEGE MUSEUM OF ART

Well, hail, Poseidon! Old mariner who was caught
Between brothers—Zeus and Hades—but
    There you are, bent
    On sinking your new trident
Into the vitals of poor Polybotes,
Who rears back upon space as if a cot
    Waited; only his shield,
    A lion, will not yield,
But, twitching its black tear-drop tail,
Glares out at us; Poseidon, hail!

On the vase's other side live three students
Dancing home, exams over, brains spent;
    Life in their heels, they clown
    The cobbled road on down
To celebrate. The central boy knows
What it is to want to *dance*, he fools and shows
    Them who is actor, they
    Are end men; so they play,
Lifting imagined wine in wassail
The students shout: Poseidon, hail!

One wed Poseidon from whom Pegasus
Sprang; no mean feat; many of us
    Know that most able horse,
    Whose love ran with the muse,
Could braid by the very rhythm of his hooves
The formal circlet this vase wears and weaves. . . .
    As to a theatre-in-the-round,
    To lives, music, sound,
How well this winejar brings us in!
Oh, navigator, hail! Poseidon!

99

Vermont Poems

A cycle

Moths in Winter

The sun,
Pied-piper this winter day,
Slants warmth in,

And up their glass-
Sheer barrier a moth
Flotilla sculls,

Tissue-paper-
Thin, shell-wings open,
As if there were

A life of days
Ahead; they sway there
Upon black ice,

While night deepens.
Colorless dancers, they long for
The shimmering neon

Inside, like divas
Drawing their wing-capes
Around them, as

Palmed against winter,
White magnets on that darkness
Of death, they falter.

Cold is the dancer.

The Snow Hole

This morning early we came straight out of the house,
Over the saddle of the nearest ridge
To catch up with a logging-road,
Then off, cross-country on our own,
On to the edge of landscape
To visit the sun.

We look ahead—ash and pine
Bristle over their summit.
The air is colder. As we climb
The sun bobs and treads ether.
Across the valley, down their great otter slide,
Utility poles are pegged one after one.

            Then at the top,
Our heads against the sky,
We see what folk tale promised:—a cleft, a seam
Of purple whiteness nailed to earth,
Sealed off from light
By barricades of stone: a deaf white shaft.
This snow will never melt. Chilled through
By now, we touch the world.

Radar and Unmarked Cars

Love at our age
  Goes far:—
    Desires:
      Unmarked cars:

Weave their way through
  The skein
    Of traffic,
      Then again. . . .

Radar:
  A sensitive
    Alignment:
      Two who love:

Gentle
  The hand upon
    The wheel:
      Communication.

To travel
  This highway
    Is intricate
      We may

Not pass
  Those unmarked cars
    Always, but our
      Radar

Will hold us true:
  We need
    Love
      At a constant speed.

Town Meeting Tuesday

Our roadside trees seem to be gathering
Their forces; just the last few days they've changed
From hibernation to life—can they feel spring
A month ahead of time? Is their sap flowing

Already? Something processional in their bearing,
A flexing of boughs, so grey and strict all winter,
An implied fullness sign this lane of tree
On tree's covenant with spring—rose, purple, sepia.

A Rune for C.

Luck? I am upset. My dog is ill.
I am now in that grey shuttling trains go in for;
The sky clouds, it is hard to believe dawn will

Ever show up. — I look for omens:
Not birds broken, not Fords lashed around trees,
But some item showing that fate is open. . . .

Sometimes, far far down in the magical past
Of us all, in something that stutters, something that rises,
There is an intimation of luck just

Swinging over our way: a cat's paw loose
In the banister a long train-run, and then,
Square and oil-shambled, blue between elms, the caboose!

Looking Up at Leaves

No one need feel alone looking up at leaves.
There are such depths to them, withdrawal, welcome,
A fragile tumult on the way to sky.
This great trunk holds apart two hemispheres
We lie between. . . . Like water lilies
Leaves fall, rise, waver, echoing
On their blue pool, whispering under the sun;
While in this shade, under our hands the brown
Tough roots seek down, lily roots searching
Down through their pool of earth to an equal depth.
Constant as water lilies we lie still,
Our breathing like the lapping of pond water,
Balanced between reflection and reflection.

Headlong

Setting off home, I ran over a woodchuck.
He lunged out — no sleight-of-wheel could have missed
His pepper-and-salt wedge head; a young fellow,
For whom the graveled roadside provided
A grainy banquet. Well, he was quite dead
When I backed up to see what I had done.

This is an old story. Only wisdom
Can read the plane geometry of this tale:
He crossing from one side of the road to the other
For nutriment. I moving out from one
Revolving crystal stage toward another,
Along a gravel road shored up by sky
Through that soft summer afternoon; just then
This headlong meeting stopped us: I ran
A gauntlet of chill air the long way home.

Running into Edgar Bellemare

In my fool seigneurial car
I came storming through dust, whirling around the corner:
Bang into skidding-distance of skidding
Bellemare, his unfledged wife, four sorry
Towheaded chicks under five, in their Hupmobile.

It amounted to little more than *Plunk:*
Their egg-shell auto crumpled. We sat on
And stared at this odd joining;
And then, unspanning, took off again
About our business. The big car pawed the road
Less mettlesomely. The Bellemares
Went on back down to find a spare fender
At Hawkes' junkyard; all of them to huddle—
Sheltered by that fender—a little longer,
Armored for life by a breastplate frailer than wishbone.

A Few Days Ago

That dark adventure was a tree,
A beldame spruce, inside whose trunk
The sap flowed secretly

Threaded to what had gone before;
Each mood or prospect had kinship
Through that slim corridor

From tap-root to leaf filament.
I found myself enclosed within
The experience. It lent

Its temper to those days, until
It was all over.—Relieved,
I moved again at will

Without that darkness ruling me,
Nor swept along in the winey sap
Of that wind-shaken tree.

What will follow? Things come upon
Us unexpectedly. I wonder
What image or condition

Will bind my next fortnight together:
The stately rising of an elm
Or sullen golden straw?

On Falling Asleep in a Mountain Cabin

We climbed together up to our mountain cabin,
Into a wooden room,
To live with the squirrels for one night.
Crickets clack-clacked, a mouse skittered;
Even the trees had disappeared, leaning to rest
On the deserted dark.

We too lay down. . . .
Under the single bulb the shadows rocked,
Our breath ballooned in the cold;
The icebox whirred: an outboard motor
Propelled us on, nearer the shoals of sleep.

One son dropped off, his faun's eyes
Leafy in the wavering light, the other lay
Brooding over a book; night lobbed
A dog's bark two miles up.
Our pine cabin was cool with the next season.
A short portage from home, we were deep in fall;
Summer, below, clear as a millpond lay—
That green expanse where we had dreamed all day.

Landscape, Deer Season

Snorting his pleasure in the dying sun,
The buck surveys his commodious estate,
Not sighting the red nostrils of the gun
Until too late.

He is alone. His body holds stock-still,
Then like a monument it falls to earth;
While the blood-red target-sun, over our hill,
Topples to death.

Late November Window

A light turns on among the trees, it glows
Through a forest of filetted bones; a lamp
Shimmers just over the carapace of the hill;
Then fades, blurs; waxes, glows.

Stars are not bright enough
To warn if the clouds reel
Awash in the firmament,
Or what ne'er-do-well in the dead
Of night is out hunting the living.

Under the phantasmagoria of sky
Our earth lies black, secret; only that brilliance
Waiting to dazzle a stag, to flash
Death in his eyes.—Oh, but that light
Has cleared our arc of trees; is it then simply
The moon out jacking deer; and fear and I?

The Dressmaker's Dummy as Scarecrow

On the hillside's upper garden a dressmaker's dummy
Is set among carrot and cress.
No longer can she swivel
In rooms that faces have panelled, eyeballs lit,
Informing stuff with her articulate line;
For an outside world she now stands sentinel
Against the crows, the shy
Foraging rodents who patter
By crisscross paths nearer by.

There is at times a blindspot in our view
When one sees nothing, is nothing, cannot see
How one has drifted here;
              At that breaking-point, one is out of place
As a dressmaker's dummy left there under the sky:
Outside, she is her livery, but changed,
Apart, surrounded by garden; the fern
At the end of perspective
Reaches now to her shoulder;
The moles are wiser and the crows are older;
She may, or she may not, outlast the winter—
The spring may find her still, and grow towards her.

A Night Picture of Pownal

FOR JFK

Thanks to the moon,
Branches of our trees are coral
Fans, cast on the lanky snow
Which, crusted though,

Takes impressions
As Matthew Brady's eye received
The desperation of Civil War;
He was its retina

And watched history
Rise and set. Above its kilt
Of steel-blue air the moon turns,
A circle leans

To stare down fissures
Of space to that black forest set
Like matchsticks on the white hillside;
All sound has died.

Our apple tree
Prints its own photograph, its strong
Branches espaliered on the snow
Fading, will not go

From our minds, the clean
Etching of dark on white, each detail
Tuned to the whole; in its precision
Enduring as bone.

What we have seen
Has become history; tragedy
Marks its design upon the brain—
We are stained by its stain.

Leaning into Light

Our hibiscus, larch,
  Marjoram, cork tree,
    Dandelion seek
      Light—
    A dull day
  Has them listless, olive-
Green, no sap running,

As I in a bad
  Time am in shadow,
    Uncertain. But then
      Light,
    Like a prophet,
  Calling them forth
To grow in the sun's great

Eye—as wisteria
  Climbs toward day—
    They revive; I have known
      Light
    Too, a presence
  One turns round to face,
Leans into and joins.

from
The Blue Garden

*for David
and for Gregory*

Away

Returning to Store Bay

Coming back to this generous island —
Shore, harbor, beach —
Is to leave behind images blown
Like cats through a shadow alley,
And the feel of cement in the teeth . . .

Returning to Store Bay
One comes back to the circular sound
Of wind whacking the scrolled
Water, the vast contest
Of undertow and surf;

To the savage ironing
Of breezes, rolling on out, stropping,

Huge in some artisan hand;
Surf and wind are round.
Whaling, pulling "back in, the water"
—In a ferryslip, wings
Of brown paper from a subway
Kiosk play hopscotch, stretch out
In gutters of that town whose
Sidewalks abrade the throat. —

Coming back to this bay
Is to meet the guffawing
Ocean, is to dance, dimensional,
Hewed out by wind, in the round,
Alive in the muscular sea.

A Letter from Little Tobago

This feeling of being alone,
    Visting all these birds who live here—
    Who are in some way our hosts—
    And who know that when night
    Falls they will be alone,

Is moving. About that unquarried quarry,
    Over its flat north rock-face,
    White Red-Billed Tropic
    Birds slant and ride out the air
    On their paper-cutter-thin tails—quarry

Of nothing because too rare; silent—
    They swoop, balance, rise, then
    Are thrown back to their grassy cliff,
    On their own, their delicate bone-
    White tails the slimmest of fans. Silent

The path we ascend; roots like lanyards
    Or narrower, saplings give us a hand,
    And we come up into birdsong—our guide
    Long part of this jungle, we two others now
    Entering: woodspeople. Lanyard

Trees thicken, stand taller; we are right
    In the forest, tuned to each bird, to noting
    The least vibration of color
    In this deep leaf-padded green-
    Yellow strangeness; careful, we move right

Toward a courtly groaning, the Birds
     Of Paradise' showy courting; they
     Display, they let drift down that
     Underwing gossamer-fall, that
     Yellow smoke, something no other bird

Has. Then Motmots, Yellow-Tails, Jacamars, — we
     Have never seen such profusion
     Before; any branch
     Can be used by the Cocrico
     As pedestal, which he takes to; we

Have lived two whole hours alone
     On the birds' own island. We have saluted
     Them by being quiet, like sensible trees;
     By being in view, they have saluted back. The
     Birds of Paradise honored us: we saw them alone,

Perched in those thickening leaves,
     Which blur, which interrupt sight;
     Now all around us birds, rocks, trees
     Know we are going, letting them
     Be, to nest as they will in their leaves.

We have boarded our dinghy and left,
     Jounced back over
     The grey mill-wheel of water;
     Forest wisdom opens on mystery;
     Mystery roofs the shy lives we have left.

Voyage autour de ma Chambre

THE HARKNESS PAVILION

Earliest of all rectangles,
    I see from my bed
A slab of building, grey out there,
    Then rose-dusted; then it's whacked
    By light, as the Arab
Sun hits it pell-mell. — A lateen
    Rig among shadows.

Becalmed in my bed,
    I wait out the tidal hours;
Nurses, from their corridor-jetty,
    Ferry forth and back
    Their soundless
Emollient nostrums; a silent
    Bell-buoy nudges the rocks

Which lie like cranked hospital
    Cots among shallows, teethed . . .
Beyond my bulrush bed, the eraser
    Sun rubs out buildings; over it an Arch-
    Bishop, tall in gauze mitre, white gown,
Leans. A Prophet? A Martyr?
    He looks down.

Wild Geese Flying

Aware at first only of the dust of sound
Drifting down to us here in the yard,
I saw him look up, searching fathoms of air
As for tidings,
Some urgent spirits' honking aloft:
Wild geese perhaps—and my eyes strained after,
Into that azure,
Then, *there* they were: *there,*
Flying in a straggle, so high, a wonder,
Glinting like wafers, silver fish-
Scales in the sun, a
Strewing of foil confetti, yet aimed;
The string of a kite's tail
Dipping, being drawn
Through that gulf stream of air
By their migrant passion;—at the edge
Of sight I still found them. . . .
Then, abruptly,
Nowhere.

The Ostrich Tree — The Palm Bird

Plunging to ground, glued
To its under-earth visions, cement brows
Clamped to soil, eyes drowned, it is anchored,
A fat truncheon.

                    Why not scale that
Leaning spine, collared
Like Venus' necklace, up, up
To where a nylon
Wind feathers-over those fat
Green eggs, and branches
Swaying all round are the nest?

Again, curving toward earth,
The grey neck hurries
To stomp
Its hoof-head down deeper; the longest ostrich,
Lacklustre, an asbestos tube, is a
Message from wind to sand . . .

We can imagine climbing, monkeylike, hand-
Over-hand
To that ostrich-frond nest;
Behind it the backdrop sky just sits
Astounded at this palm bird squawking
—In total silence—
Its Creole knowledge.

Guests

Fly in for two days;
      Unpacking loud voices from
      Matching cases, they walk all the way
      To the beach, that its surf stuns,
      Then back to relax, to order rum
      Punches;—later they nibble,

Two for the barbecue:
      Packing their plates way high
      They walk tightropes toward a table,
      Waiters bowing like surf;
      Ordering everything, rum
      Consoles them. His nibbling

Old claws knick at her one or two
      Backsides; skinny as an unpacked
      Hamper, she natters, walking crane-legged
      Through the surf of chat—
      Order amounts to unpacking—then her ruffled gross
      Grosgrained vulture's neck nods to his nickety hand.

Monkey Difference

The monkey difference
    From Catholic and
        Protestant comes down to
            Most peoples' fix on guilt . . .

A maxi-skirted papacy
    Fears female more
        Than monkey; its guillotine,
            Childbed, falls on woman

Each year . . . No monkey'd be named
    Calvin: hatred of bodily
        Love is not simian, nor the
            Puritan icehouse his,

Where a dressmaker's
    Dummy can hang
        In that abbatoir
            Till the 20th child . . .

Monkey: his simon-pure,
    Active body may be
        A hieroglyph
            For life, pinpointing

It . . . In his leaf
    Cathedral he's on his own,
        Is monkey, as long as, leaping,
            Flying, he lands — and holds on.

The Lonely Pipefish

Up, up, slender
As an eel's
Child, weaving
Through water, our lonely
Pipefish seeks out his dinner,

Scanty at best; he blinks
Cut-diamond eyes—*snap*—he
Grabs morsels so small
Only a lens pinpoints them,
But he ranges all over

That plastic preserve—dorsal
Fin tremulous—*snap*—and
Another çedilla
Of brine shrimp's gone . . .
We talk on of poetry, of love,

Of grammar; he looks
At a living comma—
Snap—sizzling about
In his two-gallon Caribbean—
And grazes on umlauts for breakfast.

His pug-nosed, yellow
Mate, aproned in gloom,
Fed rarely, slumped,
Went deadwhite, as we argued on;
That rudder-fin, round as a

Pizza-cutter, at the
End of his two-inch
Fluent stick-self, lets his eyes
Pilot his mouth—*snap* . . .
Does his kind remember? Can our kind forget?

Gold Beyond Gold

"Emeralds are green *beyond*
   Green; you look down into them
     And see the *truth* of green."

This central wreath — over
   Whose strawberry-leaves Athena's
     Heart-faced owl presides —

Is goldsmith genius, the Hellenes'
   History in art. It is a wreath-
     Symbol for Alexander, whose giant

Dream of Empire — joining
   Greece to Asia Minor — cut a swathe
     Of conquest from a route of gold.

. . . Soon, lynx, panther, griffin, ram (Darius' treasure)
   Flowered on earring, pendant,
     Belt: creatures of Dionysus, images

Of predatory urgings, fears
   Of an alloyed world,
     Alive in gold.

Herakles' knot, that amulet
   At center, frequently, of diadem,
     Thigh-band, foot-bracelet, ring,

(A reef-knot plain or garnet-studded,
   Inlaid with any treasure) — this
     Golden symbol of relationship,

They held, would heal
   Wounds; deeper than this, it stands
     For the grave, wild permanence of love.

Evening: Crown Point

Having dropped, a boiling stone,
Behind the sea, today's sun
Leaves up there a blue-black
Moiré ocean; higher,
Striations of yolk and rose; then,
Laundry-lines of silver
Strewn upon dusk.

    Into this greying
    Past, the island bats veer—
    Darting in figure-eights,
    They aquaplane on air;
    In their ballet, they skate
    Over wind-pockets, dining . . . Night
    Falls, a gavel; they have radared off.

We, on our balcony, stay on—
Above oleanders, close
To the casuarina trees which sigh
Their way to altitude. These
Grand nightfalls, splendid
As sunrise in reverse, leave us
Dark   quiet   moved . . .

Crystal-clear — Diamond-bright

As they had no ice in Tobago,
She thought it a blue shame
To see — as she cleaned up college
Rooms — all those steel-tinted ice-squares
Subsiding into drainwater. It shook her. So

She rolled tight
The rotund "cardboard-pak bag
Whose wet strength is
5½ lbs"; lugging it with
Her — baby on hip — she
Waited at the Duke Street bus-stop;
It dripped, but not much. When the bus
Hurtled up,
It clung cold to her side
Like treasure; while they stalled
In all that exhaust, she thought
About dryness in her village, Moriah,
And how only some miracle-
Magnet kept life
From falling off that

Toboggan hill. — At Main
The cool was damper. Then
Finally, out on Luck Street,
Propping open the door of
Her room — a chill still between it and her —
She was home, inside,
Alone — in a peace of crystal.

Mercedes

Hopscotch
     Through patches
     Of light, a greeneyed
Dominican slanted
     From palm-frond street-shadow in
To a job, to stay on, to be safer,
But by June, daubed soap on her mirror:
Mercedes de la Rosa está muerta

Mercedes had
     Worked Casuarina-long days:
     "San Francisco, San Francis-
     Co, San Fran . . ." written fifty-three
     Times . . . "In my grandmother's garden
Tomatoes grew, red whole
Hearts, we ate them; they said
     'Mercedes de la Rosa is dead' "

Dream-knives
     Cut out dolls—but I'll
     Help them—that leaf,
     Falling, is a dory . . .
     Chicago, Chicago;
Men: their pants
Pressed to the coil of a whip,
     Shoot billiard
     Eyes at me . . .
Merced es de la Rosa

I can hide my dolls, my
        Cuckoo-clock, though his beak
        Orders me to dance;
Sequins, I glue gold pieces, I sew
Justice on chiffon,
All colors — as I whirl,
        They dance — how my body aches!
        I must nail my cuckoo . . . The
Spinning mirror splinters:
        Mercy befits the Rose

Next day, duck with two heads,
Her radio quacked to itself; a needle
Slanted through the cuckoo's
        Heart; lint of chiffon
Rocked in Erzulie's breeze . . . "People
        Do strange sometimes," she had said,
        And,
Mercedes de la Rosa is dead

Sweet Sleep

We sleep—
After a long intractable day—
To revive, to absent
Ourselves for a bit
From responsibility . . .

. . . But there by the road at the end of the lawn,
Hatred flares up, violence sways
High as the pinetrees;

Or
The guided tour
Of an inner detective-
Story pulls us on through
Fear, crime, danger; it was all
Known before,
As if one were seeing something
Already enacted: the cliff-fall,
The revolving stairway, the moment
When cruelty shrieked, and a whole bat-
Gang swung at us, erasing
Meaning . . .

What has happened?
    Why should sleep
Be the rioting of a skiff
Over red water?
Without the liberty—
Haunted by narrative,
Eddying upon nothing,
Racked by symbols—
    To sleep?

At Mrs. Alefounder's

TOBAGO

Not perched on the top of the hill
But established there, a nest
    Leaning into a blue
    Sky, this white and blue
House is an aviary; winds live outside
And in, not knowing the difference; still,

It is a house, not quite an aviary,
Though made of porches, windows,
    Weather, verandahs, open
    To all moods of air, opening
Out on trees standing apart
Like old friends . . . Save

For the one peacock, birds
Who arrive at this giant feeder
    Come in numbers. Grasping the tilt,
    Their table, they peck—swaying as the tilt
Sways—at that mash, plump
In bill. They are outdoors, but stirred

By terrace breezes . . . The stocky Anis—
Blacker than black—drive
    Roman-nosed beaks
    At their banquet, while slimmer beaks
Of Bananaquit, Woodpecker, and the dun
Or lilac Dove, or Tanagers, sky-

Blue, cloud-white partake. The Motmot's chest
Chestnut, cap azure, each delicate
    Morningcoat iridescent, one handsome
    Jewel slotting the breast;—indeed handsome
Beyond belief, at tail's end twin prongs
Support an extra feather-inch, a test

Nature has rarely passed . . . Cocricos scamper
Pheasant-heavy, purplish, a pink wattle
    As chin, body a sturdy
    Brown; for reasons of sturdy
Attraction, an undertail fan goes orange;
They loft to a plumtree and back, trample

Their provender . . . On this balcony or off
We are outside-within an aviary,
    Free in it;—then shadow
    Tucks itself underleaf, shadow
Seines birds away, ourselves also,
As night lowers over us its abrupt snuffer.

The Cold Stones of the Moon

We pluck the cold stones of the moon
    With awkward grace,
    As if we were laying a floral
    Tribute before mankind;

We urge particles of these stones
    On anyone passing by,
    In the seeking gesture
    Of a blind man seeking alms;

We desire cold stones of the moon—
    Do they hum in frozen combustion?—
    As if luxe or love could be found
    In their cloudy crystal.

On Buccoo Reef

FOR CARL

Walked by these black oak
Legs, my mermaid hand held,
I drifted three feet over
Our coral kingdom — masked —
In the gentle, slow life
Of the reef.

Led by this dry hand
Through currents, edged past red
Stinging coral, growing
As men grow — goggled, I watched
The violet mandarin whiskers
Of a triggerfish,

His mustachioed tail . . .
And parrot- and squirrel-
Fish, eyes large as coins;
Others — an emerald triangle —
Wreathe rock and are gone . . .
Grizzled by sun,

My mermaid hand held,
Alive underwater, I saw,
Masked, their open eyes . . .
I am walked back now
Up in to air
By these oak legs.

At Home

The Blue Garden

Blue: aconite, deadly;
Iris, a grape
Hyacinth, or tulip
        Bulb lives deep
        Down under; in March
        They drill up through that frozen
            Turf. —
            Blue often reverts to magenta.

Blue: larkspur
        Sets its annual
Poisonous
Sights at six feet; — each
Year the
        Delphinium, too,
            Kills lice;
And both revert to magenta.

Blue: the delicate fringed
        Gentian is a rarity
        To be protected,
As gentian
Violet is either
        Elegance or tincture;
Still, these too can revert to magenta.

Blue: cornflowers
        Secure in their August
        Field, like bachelor's
Buttons, asters — reliable
        As wheat — return
        For their violet season;
What tone is magenta?

        It must be autumn's
        Color: camouflage: white-
Tailed deer, red maples
Drying, that brown hawk diving
        Grey as a pellet: a hodgepodge
        Of pigment; middle-
        Age has its own hue,
Which can easily revert to magenta.

        Even so, our yarn of blood
        Knits us together,
        Working
Its own narrative . . .
        This color may hold — blue
        As some eyes are — and not
Revert, but keep cobalt, cobalt.

Otis

"When King George the Fifth
Died, my cows were happy;
They needed just that sort
Of music to ease 'em down,
        Same as a person."

Our two horses enjoy
Their separate, canopied four-
Poster stalls, with silvered
Wadding run to the ridgepole,
        That Otis made them.

"Waltzes, and something soft,
Is what cows like for music;
Then they rest quiet. . . ." His sheep,
Grooming the upper pasture,
        Are belled for safety,

And their far cadence tolls
Summer's opulent hours —
While tallow fleeces thicken —
And winter's thinning days;
        "We've had a cold

Spring for eighteen years
That hasn't failed us; it's
Based on quicksand: warm
Winters, and cool in May;
        It never froze."

A wonder of nature — "wood
Splits well in cold weather" —
How things are, how things
Work, that is the study
        Of a happy man:

"Keeping animals takes
Plenty of knowing; they have
Their ways, you just must think
Quicker than they do," Otis
        Said, knowing he did.

Adam Breathing

FOR OUR DOG, SHOT BY HUNTERS

Hearing his breath, a bellows,
Fill-empty Adam's
Brown frame — he dying, perhaps,
Perhaps mending, — will air
Like a larding-needle
       Cure through him?

Listening to Adam's gospel breathing,
Raucous, impatient, while
His lungs exhort his life's
Blood to hare through the raceway
Of his body, to get on home . . .
       I wait hours

Till — hearing, quieter now,
Adam breathing, some abscess
In the heart let, some
Pegleg restored, some
Dream of the hunt expired —
       I can breathe.

Elm Burning

FOR NICHOLAS

In Zoar,
far up that hill,
Elms are burning, piled
log on log,
green, yellow,
Grey — red as a hex sign —
All sent
to their pyre, which keeps
others from sickening.
Row
On monarch
row, elms space
avenues, keep
Order in landscape, keep
the country greensilver; an elm's
Likeness is majesty; its totem
image a fountain.
Uphill
toward Zoar,
how shall our trees
be kept safe? How
Can we keep sap of our own ills
from pulsing
Bloodily as the heart?

At 79th and Park

A cry! — someone is knocked
Down on the avenue;
People don't know what to do
When a walker lies, not breathing.

I watch, 10 storeys high,
Through the acetylene air:
He has been backed up over;
Still, the accident

Is hard to credit. A group
Of 14 gathers; the Fire
Department rains like bees,
Visored, black-striped on yellow

Batting, *buzz* — they clamber
Around that globule; somebody
Brings out a comforter
For shroud; a woman's puce

Scarf bobs, from my 10th-floor view,
Desperately; by the backed truck
An arm explains, hacks air
In desperation, though no

One takes much notice. As through
A pail of glass, I see —
Far down — an ambulance,
A doctor come; they slide

Away the stretcher . . . In minutes
The piston-arm, the truck,
Puce, police, bees, group
All have been vacuumed up.

For John

The wrecker
At last pulls in;
It sizes
Up that fossil snarled
Among weeds, hunched over
Rubble ten feet down.

The wrecker's
Sure hands stalk his controls:
He has hooked a chain
Onto the rear axle, has a line from
Winch to farther wheel — leverage
In case that silly
Chooses
To blow on downhill,
Or slide off, a grouper,
Behind some ocean stone.

The wrecker plays
His crane as delicately as one tunes
A harpsichord; he has heavy prey
To land; it lifts,
          lifts just
Up
  over
     weedy roadside; then he
Lets his burden
       gently
         down.

The wreck
Sprawls like a gigged
Frog in the garage, where

The wrecker,
Sculpture in his head, burls
An edifice of bright metal:
              a perfect
Frame, in which strums his heart.

First Frost

Belatedly, I realized 1969's
First frost would change things,
Ring down a curtain of cold
To disguise our plants,

Herbs, flowers . . . Sandals
Scuffing new snow, I
Grabbed, drooped over a plastic
Bucket those vines of mini-

Tomatoes—vermillion
Spotting the snow-moth-flakes of
Our summer garden. On the laundry-
Line in the cellar, I've hung

Up, by their leaves, these white,
Green, red globules—solemn as
Kabuki dancers who bow, teeter, nod,
Awaiting a next performance.

January 26, '71

A wind-blizzard
Hurls itself screaming down,
Thieves through all corners,
Sets the old willow
To lashing itself,
Turns the grey elm's branches
To batons . . .

All our trees
Have become a febrile orchestra,
While a haze of snow speeds
Whiteness toward its barracks.

The butternut, holding up elfin
Fingers, sways, is political
On the breast of this wind;
Even a nonchalant
Bluejay zips through the
White tide with caution;

Horses are spooked—not
Knowing which side the attack
Comes from—they have windmares,
They let fly, shy, nip, buck—
Caught up in this wind-blizzard,
Forgetting the retinue
Of their day.

For Mother—A Log

ON HER EIGHTIETH BIRTHDAY
FEBRUARY 11, 1968

At twenty:
>   A girl, sun-turned,
>   Drove and knew horses,
>   Understood collie pups, and had
>   Learned what the loss of her
>   Father meant.

At forty:
>   A skipper, married,
>   She held fast to the tiller
>   Over undertows; she and Daddy
>   Loved children: she
>   Brought us together.

At sixty:
>   A woman: Daddy,
>   The anchor, gone, she
>   Caulked the whole family, cared for
>   All grandchildren, ran
>   A tight ship.

At eighty:
>   A great lady, warm
>   In the sun; thyme
>   Her perfume, nature her familiar
>   Spirit; her life alive;
>   We honor and love her.

Best of Show

Wheatfields of chiffon,
Afghans are blown
Into the ring: spunsilk
Waterfall, while

Popeyed Chihuahuas
Toothpick about, each
Radar-cocked ear
Plucking news . . . Now

Golden as carp,
Pekinese waddling
On fins of fur,
Whelk tails, swim in;

Next, the Great Danes,
Brindle or pinto,
Sleek as wallpaper,
Enter

Before feathered
English
Setters, time on their
Point to snoot

Most poodles, those
Peacock, tonsured, bright-
Eyed balls of cotton-
Candy; and

Bassets,
Paws whiter than sneakers,
Map ears their
Epaulettes; or

Weimaraners,
Coats silver
On bacon, yellow
Eyes sly; so different

From Huskies',
Whose Arctic
Look is a squint . . .
These breeds strut till,

Wheezing over its bow-
Legs, a lap
Dog trembles in:
Best of show!

Focus

Through the storm windows' double
Pane, our horses wander blurred
Like forms shivered out of old
Dice-cups. Vision flutters;
    It simmers like chestnuts
    Smoking over
Winter coals; blurred.

A shift of focus leads
To where fear starts up like decibels,
Clanging, roaring;
    Where the imagination
Skins into dark troughs, punctured
    By feared sound.
Inside the brain-pan, bells

Ring quiet away. Medically
One is not safe—the small
Cranium dwindles, almost no
Light gets in. It is as if a coconut
Shrank on itself to a golfball,
While the rioting
Of experience keeps pumping on all

Pistons: felt, understood, argued.
But later, nothing was there . . . Memory held
No more than a pin-prick, glaze
Of nothing, patting the featherbed
Into which one must have fallen
When the mind cut out light.
To the trepanned head, told

That focus will return, the shutter
Open, letting light in, that memory
Will snap back to the Judge's seat,
Condemning darkness . . . It may . . . Or
Perhaps, like a wizened
Head it will end up on Sixth Avenue,
Mincing in the breeze.

So, out of focus — ragged
Dreams, phrases — winking dull
On and off — 414-317 —
Memory chutes alongside
Happenings — disappears . . . returns . . .
Consciousness is a full
Or empty skull or grail.

Threesquare at the Landfill

Trotting, the ancient man,
like a kind kobold, veers
to help me, while Callaghan,
bluff as a mesa,

takes his time, leans
a strong hand over the broken
tailgate, reaches out all that green
plastic trove, detritus

of living, bits of tame
rubble for future lawns;
meanwhile our brown dog, Adam,
circumnavigates new territory . . .

This town dump, this Grand
Pownal Canyon, whose fortress-
nature's 'dozed from sand,
is theatre for this trio:

Adam sniffing; Callaghan
playing the real Callaghan;
Adam pausing; the old man
being a very old man.

Talking to Animals

FOR CARY

When there are animals about, who else—
People aside—does one talk to?
They form an environment of ear and eye
Most finely adjusted to turns
Of mood: terror, humor . . .

The domesticated: cats and dogs
Speak freely, handle their own
Lives, adjust our natures
To theirs and back; as cattle—
Those enormous oblongs of good-

Will—did they state their strength,
Could smash a barn a day;
As ducks in their sewing circle
Wonder, wander, flapping their
Fluent tails, as a mare

Lumbers, an iron horse on the turntable,
Setting forth a fact, while her foal's eyes dance
Like legs. Smaller creatures: four
Inches of chipmunk tell hazard
From ruin as people can't . . .

Making oneself understood
To animals—as to people—
Is a question of tone of voice,
Of communication just
Right for that neighbor;

Perhaps of being inside
A hogan, or in the middle
Of anywhere, one's antennae out,
Like my Beaver-Spirit who takes—deep
In his Eskimo ear—much wisdom from a Loon.

152

Shell

The strong delicate shell
        Of the body—shoulders
        Rising like music, subsiding,
Turning toward me like dawn—
        Arches, in warmth, a wave
        Fluted, and I rise up
To welcome the wash of the sea.

A small kettledrum, nacre,
        The slim clear heart-of-pearl
        That relays the
Ocean's tidal message,
        Meanwhile it secretes,
        As flesh does, rainbows—holds dawn in its
Curve—yet bears them within.

All these ivory breezes
        Indent the sea; and sea
        And wind thus form
A shell, or a vast scallop
        Of air and water; they meet
        Forming each other.
Shell warms; when warmed

It emerges from its resonant
        Depth, draws one to look
        Down to the whorled
Architecture of the human. Warmth is
        Kindled by touch. Into
This scalloped world we are born:
Ourselves shaped by our white housing of skin.

August

Thinking of insight,
I notice swallows
Teetering over the wire,
About to migrate;

Aware of instinct
Swaying like morning-glories
Deep-blue up there, I question
Those who lack all

Capacity for feeling,
Can't act in concert:
To fly off—? To stay—?
Flooded again

With knowledge
Of love happening, held
Onto—, transparent
With this,

I hang my life
On the brown hooks of my shoulders,
As one who comes to a well
And carries so much away.

Notes for a Foghorn

Long—short—
>Smothered
>>By air
>>>That sound

Awls
>Through a thick
>>Mist; as a hoarse
>>>*His Master's*
Voice
>Would megaphone,
>Barking
>>About reefs; or a

Cowhorn—Europa
>Lowing in minor
>>Key, dog-paddling,
>>>Lost . . . As from

A cornucopia
>Of danger, Poseidon
>>Roars, brandishes tides,
>>>The sea his cloak.

Ouroborus

With age, mind

Watches that intestinal tree:—
Throat, lung, kidney

And so forth, while I
    Eat crystals
    And they disappear;

The inside worm
    Seeks down its inner
        Telescope, chuting

Toward where heart—
    All its vivid feathers
    Dull now—takes

    Its own pulse, wonders
How much the frail.
Casing of the bowel

    Can stand today;
    Thought chutes, pulling
    Itself after itself,

Yet opts: I live, I
    Consume myself,
        I die.

For an Old Friend

FZ at 90

At peace on your porch—
    The garden
    Smouldering under the dark
    Vigil of cypress and privet—

You tell me that,
    Free now
    From desire and surfeit, you
    Can see human emotion in scale:

An Alpine relief
    Map,
    Rainbow geometry, bells
    Lunging in the Campanile . . .

This hullabaloo
    About life
    Is not my forte, you might
    Add, as I ask your blessing . . .

Brushstrokes, this green
    Wisdom,
    A vine: sitting frail in your chair,
    Towering, dispensing light.

Jim

Sat there
In a folding chair
Awaiting his father:

Sixteen
Is young, if it means
Only more beatings,

Or older
When the boy was ordered
Monthlong to his room last year—

That June crept
By in exploding slow-motion; he erupted
July 1st, like a puppy

Ran each four corners
Of the yard, while his mother's
Eyes were grey with tears . . .

Then last week his father loomed
In the doorway:—so framed,
He was shot four times;

Sound
Catapulted against the background
Hill, the slag-dark ground,

To ricochet
From that squat tannery
Which was the future.

This much older
Boy, is he in second child-
Hood now? Can he recall

More than that he sat there
In a folding chair
Waiting for his father?

Still-life: New England

From that old cow in the field
        A calf was born;
He struggles now to rise—
        No, he cannot
Yet, on his tapestry legs;
        The cow, crosshatched
With dirt, lice, underfed,
        Her cud a sour
Lozenge in her throat
        Rolls agate eyes.

Sheep with their earnest profiles
        Vaguely pit
Their muzzles at the gate,
        Wait to stampede;
If luck works for them, bars
        Will slide by their neat
Feet; grass will surround
        Them, camouflage
Through which they'll crop a path
        All through green summer.

While the boar, in the strawyard
        Of his excrement,
Tunnels, grunting through
        Each four-walled day,
The cow lies in the field;
        The calf she bore
Dies—. With what a spray
        Of whiskers, the yellow
Barncat saunters forth,
        Smells death, returns,

Prinks in the barndoorway . . .
          The cow lurches
To her feet, in need of fodder,
          Hocks trembling,
Ridgepole of hipbones slanting
          Through her canvas hide
Sharp as a longhorn's skull;
          She subsides—
Her eyes, agate no longer,
          Thicken to rubber.

Cardinal

With deep snow
    A fresh page
        Stretches
        Toward the tree-
    Line; within, a new page
Reflects the grey-white of

Ceiling; never flat,
    Snow rolls with the
        Earth's breathing—
        Slivers
    Of light, reflected,
Skate like grasshoppers

Over the whole white-
    Carpeted landscape,
        Or again, in grey
        Weather, blend into
    Dusk;—those matchstick
Trees out there, poled

Into snow, are characters
    Cutting their own shadow. My
        Page now has markings:
        Hieroglyphs of
    Talon, pen, shade,
Hoof range over this open

Country, imprint it. On snow-
    Fall—as the white
        Magic between us
        Is signed—I see
    The cardinal's red cursive
Line, written on winter, writing to spring . . .

Eight Translations

All That's To Others Pleasing, I Dislike

All that's to others pleasing, I dislike;
    The whole world brings me ennui and grief.
    —Then, what do you enjoy?—I answer, brief:
    —When each opponent makes the fatal strike:

I like to watch blows of a sword fully
    On another's face, and vessels foundering:
    To be a second Nero would be pleasing,
    And that each lovely woman should be ugly.

Amusement and good cheer I cannot breathe:
    And melancholy's what I relish most:
    All day I'd gladly follow some tomfool,
    And pay my court to sorrow for a while,
    And slaughter all whom in my cruel thoughts
    I do slaughter, there where I find death.

Cino da Pistoia
(1270–1336)

Ballade — The Hostelry of Thought

Across the forest of Delay,
By many a winding woodland route,
This present year, full eagerly,
Drawn by desire have I set out.
The aides that I despatched have sought
To find me lodging in the city
Of Destiny, and take what ought
To satisfy my heart and me,
The goodly hostelry of Thought.

And I have marshaled forty bay
Steeds, for my officers have brought
Sixty or more all told — pray
God! — and baggage-mules to boot.
If inns are wanting or all bought
Up, we will scatter readily;
Yet be it only for one night,
Whatever comes, I will essay
The goodly hostelry of Thought.

My ready funds I spend each day
In actions of some daring sort,
The which a jealous Fate who plays
Me cruelly takes in ill part.
But if my Hopes run high and straight,
And hold to what they promised me,
Such seasoned troops will I have wrought
I'll win, despite my enemy,
The goodly hostelry of Thought.

Prince, true heavenly deity,
Your grace I pray be my resort,
Until what I desire I see —
The goodly hostelry of Thought.

Charles d'Orleans
(1391–1465)

The Cats of Santa Anna

So many cats so often multiply
    They number double the stars in the Great Bear:
    Cats we observe whose coats look entirely white,
    Black cats also, and calico cats are there;
Cats with tails, and other felines tailless:
    A cat with a camel's hump I'd like to see,
    Dressed up as monkeys sometimes are, in suits
    Of velveteen: can't you find one for me?
Let mountains take care, likewise, when about
    To be delivered, that they do not bring
    Forth a mouse, who, indeed, poor fellow,
    From such a gang could never save himself.
Housewife, I warn you, keep your mind and eye
    On the stewpot boiling at the back of the stove;
    Quick, look! One's run away with the *scallopine!*
        Now I'll add the refrain:
Fully to praise this sonnet and commend,
Its tail must resemble a cat's and have an end.

Torquato Tasso
(1544–1595)

The Roses of Sa'adi

I wanted this morning to bring you a gift of roses,
But I took so many in my wide belt
The tightened knots could not contain them all

And burst asunder. The roses taking wing
In the wind were all blown out to sea,
Following the water, never to return;

The waves were red with them as if aflame.
This evening my dress bears the perfume still:
You may take from it now their fragrant souvenir.

Marceline Desbordes-Valmore
(1786–1859)

El Desdichado

The dark one am I, the widowed, unconsoled,
Prince of Aquitania whose tower lies ruined,
My one star is dead, and my radiant lute
Renders only the black sun of Melancholy.

In the night of the tomb, oh, you, my consoler,
Give me back Posilipo and the Italian sea,
The flower which delighted my desolate heart,
And the trellis where the vine and the roses marry.

Am I Eros or Phoebus, Lusignan or Biron?
My brow is still red with the kiss of the Queen;
I have dreamed in the grotto where the sirens swims . . .

And twice have I, victor, crossed the Acheron:
Passing, in turn, on Orpheus' lyre
From the sighs of a saint to a fairy's cries.

Gerard de Nerval
(1808–1855)

The Lost Wine

One day into the sea I cast
(But where I cannot now divine)
As offering to oblivion,
My small store of precious wine . . .

What, oh rare liquor, willed your loss?
Some oracle half-understood?
Some hidden impulse of the heart
That made the poured wine seem like blood?

From this infusion of smoky rose
The sea regained its purity,
Its usual transparency . . .

Lost was the wine, and drunk the waves!
I saw high in the briny air
Forms unfathomed leaping there.

Paul Valery
(1871–1945)

In the Primeval Wood

In the primeval wood
A noble tree was felled.
Vertical emptiness,
A column, vibrates there
Close to the downed trunk.

Birds, seek on, seek on,
In this tall memorial,
For the haven of your nests
So long as its murmuring lasts.

Jules Supervielle
(1884–1960)

Equestrian Statue

See how the trot endures
Between his great leap forward and my hand;
And see how firmly reined
Is the instinct to gallop away.
Because the steed that I ride
Keeps faith with a marvel:
Motionless, he, yet charged with vigor.
And thanks to how deep a calm
I possess, in bronze, my soul entire,
Serene in a chilly sky.

Jorge Guillén
(1893–   )

New Poems

Regina Coeli

This early, the small birds' trudging notes;
Six storeys high, a crane looms
        As in graceful blessing . . .
        Jay-walkers are Roman matadors,
        Charioteers drive taxis.

Past the *Palazzo di Giustizia,*
Its face being lifted, under reed awnings,
We race like dolphins through wet sound.

A new day starts up
        Through a halo of birdsong,
And I remember the *Pietà,*
She so clothed, he so naked; the withdrawn
        Young face dreaming of her old son.

        Vines branching up from each balcony,
        Flowering pots in each window, whittled-
Back plane trees shouting green;
Umbrella pines guarding old walls.

. . . My hand held to that warm cheek—
I thought of what hands were
To Michelangelo—they hold, they save;
The hand, the maker, steadiness of the heart
        —Son, my son—
Confirm direction.

The weathered church
     Jail-grey across the street,
     Wisteria everywhere
     Flowering upward
Over the lunging city—
     Pink socks on a Vespa volley off—
Our hands may be cardboard praise . . .
     Regina Coeli
     Free his youth,
     Give him grace to wake
     To a halo of birdsong!

Casuarinas

FOR LOUISE BOGAN

A woman at the window
Leans toward life in the street,
While sun plays over fire-escapes—
Piano keys—a lyric pouring
And sounding.

The wise, beautiful face
    Draws back to an Irish niche,
    Books, and the peace
    Of learning.

Casuarinas bring me Louise:
They reflect and sway,
They conjure
In triumph, near cadence.

Pride's Crossing

MAY 1st—1974

When I saw Pride
Walking on stilts beside me,
I ignored him, but

Kicked at his wooden ankles,
Ducked from his cloth
Eye. He moved ahead. I fell

Back to my coral garden,
Where life glows.
Coming on up

From that Indian-carpet floor,

I watched Pride dancing like Icarus,
Teasing the sun. I fled by a plummet
Of lemmings. Once home—

I fastened white strings of my denim
Sack above; a tiara. I crumpled.
Silence. Then iron Pride

Like a trolley rolled over two pins,
Forming inch-scissors: a cross-road . . .

for Genoveva Forest de Sastre
and for Kitty Genovese

Haitian proverb: "The pencil of God has no eraser."
   Robert Burns: "Man's inhumanity to man . . ."

Is ineradicable; cruelty adds inches
To the Falange boot,
To brass-knuckled hatred
Of Genoveva's human-kind.

Kitty, sensing the pad of feet, the jackknife,
Screamed up to those empty cubes
Where people, lacquered by television-
Crime, were deaf. Each one.

How can I reconcile thoughts of
Kitty, Genoveva with myself—
One dead, one dying, one safe still,
At work on language?
If you *know* this sorrow, it breaks the heart
Apart like a split cabbage.

The Mirror

FOR DAVID

The mirror reflects what it must reflect:
    A Bavarian room, hiking-shoe colored,
    The dirndl-lampshade on its weighted
    Chain; sallow walls stare at that glass
    which holds all in place.
If this mirror, in its curlycued gold,
    Had a counterpart
    Across the room,
    They would — while Sunday bells toss high
    Alpine cadenzas —
See deeply. I look in your eyes,
    Reflections combatting,
    Mingling. Is the future shown there also,
    Also in place?

Time

May inch; or fall headlong
to splash through night,
drowning all rhythm.

    At times,
our day struggles one yard ahead:
Inner pedometer footless,
we grey with sloth, the heart cold as a trashcan,
around whose silver flutings we coil—
while the boisterous world
thrashes, gauze-miles away.

    At others, streamlined through hours
which escape backwards,—
faces caught for an instant
in the opposite train—
we know one more day year has careened by,
witless as a balloon.

Sometimes, armed with love, the pace
    is just right, night comes when
    it should, after the day's chorale.
We have met again, and meet again
life's colors.

Man With Violin

FOR M.W.

Under a combed-pine ceiling, a maze,
   The man with violin
Tunes his thought and plays

Arpeggios in red flight. His heart's
   Busy, musical memory
Prompts us to set

Up a portrait of one
   Who knows his world, all delicate
Art's rivalry, and hurricane;

Who knows, with a farmer's true sense,
   The stance of a prime Jersey —
True music, true fond silence.

Cricket Raft

Thoth, let us write out
    Our Book of the Living,
As we should: it is about
    The trend down-river,
The coming-forth-by-day.

    As I swim, the sun claims
Its horizon. Crickets
Are blown in; they board
    Each his leaf-raft,
    And just may leap
To shore. Crickets, myself,
With hope, will come, then,
    Forth by day.

2nd Wind

My son's house
    Up on our hill,
Looks out, over my shoulder;
Its barn-cabin being
    Takes to a scudding wind.

It looks away at land
    Roiling under white cover,—
Tree-banks massive as dinosaurs
Smoothing to field; snow-squalls.
    Drummed by a wild wind

I look up at
    This edifice tuned
By twenty years green
Learning. Across the valley
    An iron flurry speaks.

As my son's house
    Looks far, it is
Seasoned, there; from this proud
Young life a seconding
    Wind breathes through me —

And I accept
    My autumn wandering,
Winter, June's
Skeleton summer . . . Now
    So blows, now, my 2nd wind!

For Stewart P. Park: 1907–1976

A Grandfather Clock
Stands; in humane
Script, morning-glories
Flute out from their heartwood center,
Shape what it was and is.

The pendulum, a brass pulse,
Goes its reflective, rural way,
Steadying; it leans toward change,
It leans toward years past . . .

This polished wood
Artifact has had so many days
When eyes looked straight for guidance—
Now the tall paneled form
Looms there, striking our memory,
But the face is gone.

A Parable

Bluely innocent, the pool
Absorbs attention. I dive,
Metaphorically, from a 2nd-storey
Window; it draws me down.

Here is water, covered by air,
Resting on earth; fire
Supplied by the sun; a sundial
Watching each day.

     Kindling of bone—
words reveal us—our backbone.
     They are our structure:
Language makes dimness real;
     Stupidity real;
It makes a concordance of love.

What is a parable?
     It is wandering,
Reclining bluely. It is a theory
Of blueness, of energy, likes words growing
Weeds, antlers . . . It is the pool.

"The Sixth Color of the Afternoon"

Not long from the sea, Venus
Steps forward to her rock,
In a garden of rainbow flowers.
These elements: a broad-based
Body—statue aslant
But balanced—in one hand holding
A half-furled wave, her robe, its rough
Profusion widening.
The golden apple she had won
From Paris fecund in her palm.

At that moment of change
To the fourth color of the afternoon
The apple sun had blazed, the garden
Flowers brimmed with light. The old man,
Hand tied to its wand, pointed to faults
Which faded with each gesture, as at creation
Adam was thought and formed.

All art
Lies in that hair-headdress, crowning the naked
Woman, rippling, classic, curling
Back to the knot, one scroll escaping;
The bird-wing mouth, inward eye secure.

At the sixth color of the afternoon,
We range about her as a mirror—
Her symbol—and she exists inside our eyes,
Morning star at evening. To the old man
She meant: "This is as it should be. I am here."

Written for the presentation of the first casting of Renoir's "Venus" to the Clark Art Institute, Williamstown, Massachusetts.